MIDNIGHT SUN

and Other Stories of the Unexplained

WI

MIDNIGHT SUN

and Other Stories of the Unexplained

EARL P. MURRAY

A TOM DOHERTY ASSOCIATES BOOK
NEW YORK

For Eleanor Rigby and everyone like her . . .

Design by Jane Adele Regina

A Tor Book
Published by Tom Doherty Associates, LLC
175 Fifth Avenue
New York, NY 10010

www.tor.com

Tor® is a registered trademark of Tom Doherty Associates, LLC.

ISBN 0-312-87362-X

First Edition: October 2000

Printed in the United States of America

0 9 8 7 6 5 4 3 2 1

Contents

Introduction   7

PART ONE

Midnight Sun   13
The Honeymoon Lodge   41
The Mysterious Garden   57

PART TWO

The Dark Angel of Texas   77
The Valley of Witches   87
The Shadow in the Park   97
The Old Man and the Crow   105
The Large Winged Shadow   117

PART THREE

The Dark Game   133
The Eyes in the Shadows   145
The Rat Room   157
Screaming in the Rain   171

Index   187

Introduction

It isn't always advisable to explore the unknown. Especially when what awaits you there can turn your mind inside out.

And leave you wondering if you can ever escape the memory.

The stories in this volume describe a realm that lies beyond ordinary understanding. They are stories of individuals, and groups of people, who's lives have been forever affected by paranormal events. In some cases, the individuals wished to tell their story, with no fear of being classified as abnormal. Others wished to remain anonymous.

None of them suffer from delusions or hallucinations, or any form of mental illness. They are ordinary people living, for the most part, everyday lives that somehow came in contact with the realm of the unknown. They discovered a part of themselves, or a connection outside of themselves, that suddenly brought them to attention.

In each case, the events portrayed are so unusual to the average person that the credibility of such a circumstance must come into question. But as our technology and scientific boundaries expand, we are beginning to see and understand many concepts that at one time could not even be imagined.

Still, there are some events in our lives that science, as a form of literal understanding, may never touch.

Past lives have always been a controversial subject. No one is certain how to explain the phenomenon. Questions as to the evolvement of the soul toward God arise, and how each individual's journey is different, yet in many ways the same, as another's.

Is it possible that we could have been in another body at another time in another place? Even in another century? Or even before recorded time itself?

And if so, why?

There are those who are convinced of that fact, and more are joining their ranks on a daily basis. They see it as an answer to the process of growth and understanding within humankind. A journey, or process, of discovery that leads eventually to the true source of all life, a final connection to all living things.

Certainly a link to that which we seek answers to is our inner dream world—a mirror of what we want to know, or need to know, about ourselves and our surroundings. It happens to all of us. We fall unconscious and see things through a different perspective. We want to know what it all means.

It makes us very nervous and we want to know, most of all, why we are so afraid of that learning.

For those who have told their stories here, fear has certainly gripped them at the deepest level. What came to them came unannounced, and not always of an innocent nature.

The Ouija board is not a toy. In the hands of the curious, or those seeking power, it can lead to a dark realm of disaster. When certain doors are opened, unwanted visitors are sure to enter.

Within some of these stories are dark, sooty figures that are beckoned to or otherwise allowed into a room by a person or persons experimenting with danger. Others enter a state already created by someone before them and find themselves victimized by something unspeakable.

The same can also be said of delving into cultural norms where the investigator either has no knowledge on any level of what they are seeking, or no respect, or both.

The world of native spiritualism and mythology is a place of strange and often deadly secrets. To enter here is to step into a time and place that has no boundaries, and takes no prisoners. Should you seek in good faith, and you are on the right pathway, there can be spiritual knowledge gained. But you must know your own limits or that world will swallow you whole.

In these pages you will see unusual things through the eyes of those who lived the events. Whether a name has been changed or a group of events, similar in nature, have been condensed into a single story does not alter the facts, the truth of the ordeal, or the questions that linger in the minds of those who experienced them.

Besides those who have been shown the sensitive and demanding interior of Native American mysticism, there is a woman and a man who still live with characters from the early West, and a woman who met the widowed spirit of a U.S. Cavalry soldier from the last century.

And in addition to those who have been terrorized by Ouija board activity, you will meet an unusual man who's entire life, even into his deepest nighttime existence, was geared toward reaching Alaska. He had no idea for what purpose until one strange night high upon a mountain pass when a bad storm led him into a realm of mystery that will forever leave him wondering.

We owe a debt of gratitude to those who have opened themselves here. We see, through their strange journeys and often horrifying encounters, that there are mysterious powers and secrets that can influence us for the rest of our lives. With their stories they teach us that we best be aware at all times of that which we don't understand. We must be careful where we enter, what we seek, and how we seek it.

Earl P. Murray
Fort Collins, Colorado

PART ONE

Midnight Sun

I

Chilkoot Pass
Klondike, Alaska

Carl Reese grew up in suburban Seattle, his thoughts and
dreams always reaching northward toward Alaska. While
still in high school, Carl thought about ways to see the huge
state that hails itself as America's last great wilderness. A trip
or vacation might satisfy some of his interest, but he believed that he needed more than just a short time there.
Besides, his parents rarely took time off from their work to
relax.

Despite that, Carl thought of ways that he might make
his intense desire real. The pipeline; fishing boats; it all came
to mind, but he didn't believe that a regular job was the
means by which he could satisfy his hunger.

"It was impossible for me to understand at the time,"

Carl explains. "I was always so drawn to the far north. It was in my blood somehow. Even as a small boy I felt that I just *needed* to get there. I needed to experience the place in some way that I couldn't fully comprehend, except that it was an intense hunger on some level."

As a small boy, Carl often awakened in the middle of the night crying. While his mother soothed him, he talked about his "snow dreams" and the feeling that he was lost in a swirling storm but didn't want to move because he would find himself in a bad place. He knew for certain that he was in Alaska, the far north of Jack London, his father's favorite author.

Carl had heard Jack London's stories read to him many times, and felt that he somehow knew the places in those tales. He asked his father to read from other authors, anyone but Jack London. He told his father that he was tired of the stories when in reality, he was mesmerized by them, and frightened at the same time.

This caused a separation between Carl and his father.

"He saw it as a rejection of his attempt to bond with me," Carl says. "He wanted me to relate to his personal connection with the wilderness, which I did, but he didn't understand that there was something about the stories, yet not really linked to the stories themselves, that was terrifying me. As a result, he began to see me as a sissy, or a weakling of sorts."

The snow dreams continued, never nightly, but just often enough to remind Carl that they would never go away—year in and year out, just often enough to make it difficult to concentrate on the things a boy wants to do.

Now distanced from his father, he gravitated toward his mother.

She could do nothing for Carl, either. Despite her repeated attempts at convincing her son that the dreams were nothing more than a child's nightmare, young Carl continued to go deeper and deeper into the dreams and farther into his fear. He repeatedly asked his mother what he might do to avoid going to the "bad place."

"I wanted to know how to get out of the storms," Carl recalls. "I always asked her if there was a way out of the snow without going straight ahead. I knew that if I went to one side or the other, I would get lost and freeze to death, and that straight ahead would be a place of warmth, but I still didn't want to go straight ahead. It was driving me crazy, literally."

Taking young Carl to a counselor proved to be of no help. The counselor agreed that the Jack London stories had instilled a lot of fear in the boy, something that would now be difficult to remove. This further alienated him from his father, the one individual who could be of the most help at this time in his life.

From the time he was old enough to walk, Carl was drawn to the great outdoors. His father, an adventurer in his own right, had grown up in northern California and was adept at hiking and rock climbing. Carl took readily to these and other outdoor sports and in his early teen years worked to gain his father's good graces back by lying about his dreams and getting back into the Jack London stories.

And the more he read the stories, the deeper he fell into his fear.

That fear deepened when he stood out in his first snowstorm.

He was a freshman in high school, hiking a trail through the Cascade range with some friends. Prior to this he had never been in the mountains so late in the year, and the high snowfields he had encountered in the summer had been old snow, lying dormant, not moving, as it always was in his dreams.

"I wanted to run for my life," Carl remembers. "The guys with me were laughing and opening their mouths to take it in, but all I could think about was screaming and running. But, somehow, I kept my composure."

Carl now became determined not to give in to his fear. He would find as many storms as he could and he would challenge them to take him, wherever it was they wanted to take him, deep into some strange mode of horror that no one but he could understand.

And since there was no escape, driving his mind and body toward athletic perfection would be his choice of preparation.

He began building himself for the challenge by working on his physical stamina. He spent hours on end cross-country bicycle racing and trekking long distance through the mountain ranges of Oregon and Washington with high school friends. He even spent part of a summer in the majestic Sierra Nevada range, where his father had hiked and camped during his younger years.

With his father's blessing, Carl enrolled in a summer

camp in the Sierras for wilderness training. He passed with flying colors. He pushed himself well past the limit, insisting on remaining out an additional day on his own, at the end of a survival test, eluding the instructors to prove that he could do it. The instructors considered sending him home, but he begged them to understand his reasoning. He had been raised to prove himself continually and this was just a result of that drive.

After that experience, Carl Reese never looked back, but continued to test himself, on his own and with others. It became a game of sorts with him, to see if he could get his father's approval as a risk taker and survivor. Challenging the great outdoors by taking chances on rock-climbing trips and during boat and rafting outings became the rule rather than the exception.

All the while, he still continued to be plagued by his snow dreams. The more he challenged them, the more intense they became.

"My idea of charging through them backfired," Carl explains. "The feeling of foreboding grew deeper, and as I grew older I got to the point where I was afraid to go to sleep."

Carl's mother saw her son drawing ever closer to a nervous breakdown and insisted he try counseling again. He met with a psychiatrist who, after several visits, proclaimed that he was suffering from a neurosis caused by a deep-seated fear of becoming an adult. This was not specific enough and made little sense, as few teenagers express a desire to leave that last link to early life. As a result, the counselor couldn't help Carl reach that fear, nor could the next counselor, a middle-aged woman who told his parents that they should seek someone well versed in astrology, the dealings of people's lives with regards to star and planet alignments at the time of birth.

That course of discovery, she promised them, would bring the fear to the surface and show it for what it really was, not just what it seemed to be.

"Of course, my parents thought she was crazy, and told her as much," Carl recalls. "They just put me on sedatives, at the instruction of the first counselor. But medication didn't work; it just made my dreams more vivid and filled with sparkling lights instead of just regular color. I stopped taking pills and once again stopped talking about the dreams, and my parents never knew the difference."

Meanwhile, Carl continued to pursue his avid interest in hiking, fishing, and outdoor activities, talking more and more about doing something for a living that would allow him to stay in the mountains. As a result, Carl's future was something he argued with his family about a great deal. His father, a successful real estate broker in California, and then in the Seattle area, urged Carl to pursue the same career, after getting a business degree from a respected university. His mother, a successful lawyer in the real estate field, agreed.

But Carl balked at their suggestions. He felt inclined toward a nomadic life, possibly as a ski instructor or a back-country tour guide somewhere. He had never been able to talk his parents into an Alaskan vacation and had decided that now that he was an adult, he could make his own decisions.

Carl was told if he decided to pursue his fantasies, he would have to do it on his own, and at his own expense. With everything in life handed to him prior to this, he was ill prepared to step out into the world on his own.

His take on the fast lane varied between amusement and frustration. The modern world of the mid-1980s required a total commitment toward financial gain if any kind of cultural expectations were to be met, and his parents certainly expected him to strive toward that end. But his hopes and his dreams, the good ones as well as the bad ones, kept pulling him toward the north.

II

During Carl's senior year in high school, after a series of tense and lengthy discussions, he agreed to enter business school and pursue his outdoors interests on the side. He was accepted at the University of San Francisco, his father's alma mater, and began his studies there.

During his sophomore year, he met Sally Bridges, a history major with emphasis on the transcontinental migration west during the nineteenth and early twentieth centuries.

In addition, she had an avid passion for discovering Alaska.

The two fell in love immediately. Not just with one another, but also with the combined excitement over reaching the vast wilderness of the forty-ninth state.

"It was a perfect combination," Carl remembers. "The only thing that came between us was my risk taking. Sally was very conservative and down to earth when it came to safety. She got angry with me a number of times."

Sally's brother, Mark, was studying forestry at Oregon State University and shared Carl's enthusiasm for testing the odds in the high country. Sally thought them both a bit crazy when it came to reaching the next peak no matter the time of day or night, or skiing off the face of a steep mountain with nothing but rocks along the slope below them.

"I knew they were kindred spirits of a sort," Sally says, "just like Carl and I. But I didn't share their passion for risk. They both seemed to want to push the limit when it came to defying death."

Despite his love for Sally, and her constant display of affection and respect for him, Carl just couldn't stay away from danger. His continual urge to tempt fate seemed to be growing ever stronger, not diminishing.

It didn't stop even when Mark tore up his knee and broke both arms in a skiing accident. Carl continued to ski off dangerous precipices, and also took up sky diving and hang gliding. But he finally agreed to give it all up at Sally's request.

"She told me that she refused to be a widow," Carl tells. "She had accepted my proposal for marriage, but didn't feel she could go through with it if I insisted on taking unnecessary risks."

Carl had a difficult time being sedentary. In anyone else's frame of reference, he was still a risk taker, but not at his previous level. He still pushed himself to the limit in his physical training and took chances in the backcountry, including a dangerous march through a herd of bison in Yellowstone Park, just to see what they would do.

"I'll admit," Carl says, "I wasn't really playing with a full deck in those days. Maybe it was because of my dreams. I couldn't get them out of my mind and I guess I just wanted to do something to change that."

When a Yellowstone ranger took him aside and described what a bull bison can do to a human being, Carl began to get the picture.

"He impressed upon me that nature is nothing to take chances with," Carl recalls. "I'd lived outdoors most of my life but I had never appreciated the value—I had always viewed the backcountry as a challenge."

At Sally's request, Carl pursued counseling once again. This time, though, he took a different route. Remembering what the second counselor had told his parents during his teen years, he sidestepped the traditional approach and sought out a spiritualist.

He found Dr. Martin Solberg, who practiced in San Francisco and came highly recommended. In addition to specializing in modern psychology, Dr. Solberg had added the specialty of working in past life therapy, something relatively new and highly controversial.

"Dr. Solberg told me at the onset that whether I believed in the work or not, it would help me," Carl remembers. "He suggested that I throw any preconceived notions away and just go through with his instructions. I was amazed at some of the things I discovered."

Dr. Solberg was somewhat puzzled by Carl's unusual storm phobia and his recurring dream, but believed that together they could find the source of the problem. He took Carl through a series of sessions during which a number of interesting visions came to him, which he insists were definitely not imagined.

"I know the difference between what I can bring to myself as a picture and what comes to me without prior envisioning," Carl insists. "What I went through was certainly something that I didn't bring out on my own."

Carl remembers a session where Dr. Solberg helped him into a relaxed state and asked him to stroll along a pathway lined with trees and then out into a meadow filled with fog. In the meadow, he was asked to stand still while the fog lifted.

Carl went through the experience, reliving something he couldn't understand.

"As soon as the fog cleared and I could see, I noticed that I was in the middle of a battlefield, and that my blue uniform had a red stain in the stomach area. I couldn't feel any pain or anxiety, but I knew that I was dying and that I didn't want to."

While still in the meadow, holding his stomach, Carl walked past dead and dying soldiers, trying to catch up to the fight, which was moving downhill from him into another area.

"There was a lot of screaming and crying all around me," Carl recalls. "Mayhem, pure mayhem. I knew that I had grown up in Missouri and that I was into my second year of fighting for the Union and that everything we did and all that we talked about was for the Union cause. I realized that it was the same on the other side, within the Confederate lines. I had talked with some of their soldiers the night before the battle, while we were all getting water from the same creek. One of them had looked at me and told me that he would meet me above the field the next day."

During Carl's walk to try and catch up with his fellow soldiers, his vision grew blurry and he lost strength quickly. He sat down and leaned back against a tree. His entire front was a mass of blood.

"I looked up," Carl says, "and saw that the air immediately above the battlefield was filled with white forms that hovered, some of them crying out. I realized that they were the spirits of the dead, wondering what to do or where to go. It was so strange, because I felt myself lifting out of my body and joining them. I looked back and saw myself against the tree, my head bowed over to one side and my arms loose at my side."

Stranger yet, Carl says, was rejoining the Confederate soldier he had met at the creek the night before.

"He was there, in the air beside me. I didn't see him as a body, but I felt him. I knew who he was and I realized that he and I had been friends somewhere, in another time and place. And he told me that we had to go and that the world as we knew it no longer held any meaning.

"I had worried about my wife and infant son, but he told me that they would survive and that I would have to trust that their lives would go the way they were supposed to. Then I remember leaving with him, and some others, ushered toward a brilliant light by men dressed in all manner of uniforms, from ancient Rome and Greece and the Revolutionary War, clear up through World War I and II, and even Vietnam. So very strange, because those wars had yet to be fought—that time had not even come into being yet."

Shaken by the experience, Carl Reese began to realize that, indeed, the world as he had come to know it might not be anything close to the reality of the life of the spirit. He wanted to think that the experience as a dying Union soldier, and another experience as an aristocrat dying by the guillotine in revolutionary France, had all been scenes from books he had read and that he had just formulated the images in his mind.

Still another session took him to the deserts of Arabia and a bizarre experience as sultan's daughter. Though the eyes of a woman, the blistering hot sand was very real, as were the nomadic raiders that captured him and, within a short time, had abandoned him in the desert, fleeing from the sultan's soldiers.

Such dramatic pieces of time and seemingly a life that had belonged to him couldn't possibly be real.

But he believed they had been. These images, loaded with a strong realization of the times and the state of the country, could never be absorbed from a book, and could never be just thought up.

No, these experiences had to have been lived, he decided, by whomever he was deep inside.

Perhaps his own soul?

"I still don't know how it works," Carl confesses. "I knew all there was to know about being a Union soldier, though had never studied the Civil War to any extent. And I knew everything there was to know about the battle and it's aftermath. It all came to me during that session with Dr. Solberg. It was the same with the other sessions: I *knew* all about the times and the people and the events. It was as if I had been living there and then."

Carl discussed it with Sally and the two agreed that something very difficult to comprehend had taken place, and that there would surely be more unexplained events to follow, whether or not he continued working with Dr. Solberg.

Their prophecy came to pass quickly and as Carl Reese soon discovered, he had suddenly begun an extraordinary journey toward the great state of Alaska.

III

Carl and Sally were married in the spring of 1988. That fall they shared their first unusual experience together.

It occurred on a camping trip in the mountains above the Big Sur area of California. After Thanksgiving turkey with Sally's family, they decided to take the rest of their break from college to trek though the woods.

A blustering wind arrived just after midnight and Carl woke up in the middle of one of his snow dreams. He left the tent and wandered for a time. When he finally returned, Sally was beside herself, calling out to him.

"I was scared to death," she remembers. "I had no idea where he had gone and he wasn't answering me. It wasn't like him at all. He'd done a lot of crazy things, but nothing like this."

What Carl remembers is that he had looked out of the tent into the storm and had felt they must get out of the area or die.

"I was sure that we were going to be snowed in and trapped until spring," Carl tells. "I shook Sally but she wouldn't awaken. When I went outside the tent, I guess I just started walking in my sleep. That's something I never do, so I was amazed that I had been gone for nearly half an hour and then, somehow, managed to find my way back."

The rest of Carl's memory regarding that night was hazy. But he realized something very strange had happened, and that he had seen other people during his wanderings.

"One of them was laughing at me," Carl tells. "I tried to reach him, to make him stop laughing, but he stayed just out of reach. There were others watching. I couldn't put it together and I didn't know what it all meant."

The following spring, Carl would finally discover what that dream was all about, and how it tied into his nightmares of the snowstorm.

Carl and Sally sat in a Skagway, Alaska, museum, listening to a lecturer discuss the Alaskan gold rush of the late 1800s and early 1900s. They had decided to spend spring break from college in the Klondike, seeing the rugged country and learning what they could about the area.

They had been making plans since Christmas, when they had opened presents and discovered that each had given the other the same gift: An envelope filled with pictures of Alaska and a letter of invitation to partake in an adventure.

"That was so unusual in itself," Carl says. "I had decided to write Sally a note inviting her to join me in Alaska, and had collected some pictures. She had decided to do the very same thing. Her pictures were different than mine, but the letters were so similar that it was eerie."

Carl still laughs at their total surprise in discovering one another's envelope under the tree.

He continues: "Of course everyone thought we'd planned the invitations together. No one believed that neither of us knew what the other one was up to. I doubt if they'll ever believe it."

Two friends from college had joined them: Bob and LeAnn Gibson, a married couple Sally had met in one of her history classes. Sally had talked it over with Carl and they agreed that another couple could be fun, especially those two, who enjoyed the outdoors as much as anyone could.

Bob had been to Skagway before, and also Dawson City, all during the previous three years. He had gathered a lot of information on the Klondike gold rush and had been wanting to gather more, which he intended to use for a master's thesis some time in the future.

Both couples had finished final exams early and they had gotten off to a good start on their excursion. They flew to Anchorage and then on to Skagway, where they planned to snowshoe and cross-country ski their way along the Chilkoot Trail toward Dyea, a major gold camp during the boom era.

When they had first reached Skagway, Carl had commented that maybe they shouldn't make the trek toward Dyea. It happened in their hotel room as they were preparing to join Bob and LeAnn for dinner.

"It was so unlike him," Sally remembers. "He had been looking forward to the trip for so long, and then to say, 'Let's forget it,' really shocked me."

Then, just as quickly, Carl was back to being eager to get on the trail.

"It seemed to me like he didn't even remember that he'd suggested not going through with it," Sally tells. "He was putting on his coat and I asked him why he hadn't wanted to go, and he turned and gave me a blank stare. It was truly confusing."

At dinner, Carl commented that they would be seeing places that hadn't changed since the gold rush. Bob had studied the area extensively for the work he would be doing as a graduate student in history and had marked some places down on a map.

Carl took an active interest in a spot not far off the Chilkoot Trail just below the pass.

"I thought it would be interesting to investigate an area where it was said that Jack London had been," he says. "I had reread all of London's stories since Christmas, just to get back into the mood for the trip."

Strangely enough, he hadn't experienced any of his snow dreams. He hadn't experienced one in nearly six months.

"I had gotten the best sleep of my life during that time," Carl says. "But right after Sally and I had finished dinner with Bob and LeAnn, it began to snow, and I knew that the time of no dreams had ended.

That night, with Sally sleeping soundly beside him, Carl tossed and turned, trapped somewhere in a storm that was worsening, holding him fast within a realm of terror stronger than any he had ever known.

Still, he didn't remember the evening before, when he had told Sally that their journey along the Chilkoot might not be a good idea.

"I awakened in the morning with sweat dripping off me," Carl recalls. "That never happens, as Sally and I both like sleeping in a cool room. We even had the window cracked a bit and it was actually quite chilly."

Sally realized that he had experienced another dream and said something to him about his comment regarding their trip. Carl told her that he'd never said it. He was convinced that he hadn't entertained the thought at all, that he would never share a fear like that with anyone, not even Sally.

Carl told her that, in fact, he was very interested in making the trip over the Chilkoot, an experience he had been looking forward to for a long time.

———

Bob had been interested in taking in the lecture that morning of their departure, but Carl was eager to leave and get started on their adventure. He didn't think the talk was that stimulating and whispered as much to Sally a number of times. Outside the museum, he said that they should be getting ready to start their trip and not waste their time on someone who had really never seen what it was really like to yearn madly for gold.

"I told Sally, and Bob and LeAnn as well, that I couldn't believe that the lecturer had any real sense of what happened in the gold fields," Carl remembers. "He just didn't convey it to me."

At this point Sally began to worry. She had begun to notice subtle things in Carl's behavior that suggested to her that he might be regressing into his old, chance-taking behavior.

"There was no doubt in my mind that Carl was going to do something off the wall," she remembers. "I could see it in his eyes. I tried several times to talk to him about it but he just brushed me off."

Carl doesn't remember himself falling back into the old patterns.

"At the time, I couldn't see what she was talking about and I didn't believe her. We argued, even in front of Bob and LeAnn. I guess I really wasn't aware of some realities that would present themselves later."

IV

Their adventure started out on a high note. They were well prepared for winter travel and camping, each couple having been on various excursions of their own. They just hadn't camped together and though things went smooth during the first day, by the end of the second, some tensions began to grow.

"Bob was just too conservative for me," Carl tells. "There were some good slopes to ski down but since we were on cross-country skis and not the regular, broader, downhill version, he didn't want to take any chances."

On the other hand, Carl had no problem taking off over a steep bank and after having his fun, traversing the slope back up at an angle, a process that took up a lot of time and soon wore on Bob's nerves.

In addition, their camps were, to say the least, bizarre. Carl would push them to go farther than anyone else wanted to, insisting that the late sun gave them a lot of good light for travel. And once in camp, he would wait until the sun had crested and rustle everyone out to view the northern lights.

Though everyone else wanted to get what sleep they could, Carl wasn't interested in his sleeping bag. He was having his snow dreams in living color and wandering outside the tents, much the same as he had in the Sierras some years before.

"A lot was going on inside me and I couldn't bring

myself to face it," Carl remembers. "Once again, I was trying to run away from it and it just wasn't working."

Finally, Bob called a camp discussion, where everyone brought their feelings out. No one yelled and no one got overly angry, mainly because Carl never argued one point about his behavior. He voiced that he saw nothing wrong with it, but he didn't argue.

Sally, caught in the middle, apologized over and over to Bob and LeAnn, who insisted that she not worry about it. These things sometimes happened.

When the discussion were over, it was decided that they would finish their trek to the top of the pass and then return to Skagway for an earlier flight out. Bob was no longer interested in going all the way to Dyea.

Carl now began to argue, insisting that the best part of the trip lay on the other side of Chilkoot.

"I know he thought I was crazy," Carl says. "He'd been over there and I hadn't. I just believed it to be true, based on eavesdropping I had done in Skagway."

If Bob agreed with Carl, he didn't say so. Nothing mattered to him at that point but getting back home. Perhaps he should have picked better camping partners.

They camped on the pass with a small pack of wolves. Carl sat up and watched them while everyone else, exhausted from the climb, buried themselves in down sleeping bags.

Even after a third cup of coffee, Carl slumped over in sleep. Within his field of dream vision, there was no place to go. The storm had started and the air was filled with soft, feathery flakes that drifted to the ground like loose cotton. In his dream the place ahead of him, the dark place where he had to go, was every bit as foreboding as in any dream he had thus far experienced. But this time he would go there.

He was suddenly awakened by Sally's firm shaking. She wasn't happy with him and insisted that he come to bed.

"She said that it was our last night and that we should get some good rest to be able to start back in the morning," Carl remembers. "She was depressed over my behavior and angry at the same time. I didn't know what to tell her."

Sally finally fell asleep but Carl couldn't. He didn't want to face the dream again.

In addition, a strong sense of urgency was pulling him outside the tent.

He dressed quietly and when he got outside, it was snowing—soft, heavy flakes, like cotton.

He put on his snowshoes and started down the other side of the pass.

"I will never be able to fully explain what happened that night," Carl tells. "I only know that I somehow believed I was inside my dream and going into that dark and dangerous place I had been avoiding all my life. I wanted to face whatever it was that awaited me. I wanted to either die or get it all resolved."

In his mind, Carl Reese knew why he had come to the Klondike, and why he was now wandering in a blinding snowstorm just below Chilkoot pass.

"It all happened very fast after I got started," Carl recalls. "I kept walking and I was certain I was so lost that I would never find my way back to camp. That's when I saw the light and heard the piano music."

A short ways ahead, Carl discovered a large log cabin, two-story in design. On the leeward side of the storm a team of dogs lay nestled under a pile of hides and blankets. Barking could be heard coming from inside the cabin.

Before Carl could knock an older man opened the door and laughed, saying, "I've seen some crazy ones come over that pass, but you're the craziest. This time of night, in this weather? You're the craziest."

The laugh bothered Carl. He had heard it before, he knew, but couldn't remember where.

Inside, it was warm and a large lady dressed in a dark and greasy woolen dress was playing a piano in the back of the first floor. There was laughing and yelling upstairs, where a number of people occupied a large, open balcony. Two men were tying a wooden sign across the railing at the top of the stairs. One of them, a large man with wild blue eyes, was putting the finishing touches on the letters with a large knife. The sign read:

WELCOME TO THE
MIDNIGHT SUN

The old man laughed over and over and handed Carl a shot of rye whiskey mixed with honey and water.

"He told me that I needed my bones warmed," Carl tells. "Then he said that I had come to the wrong place and laughed again."

Carl asked the man what he meant by the "wrong

place," and he pointed upstairs to where the wild-eyed man with the knife was watching him. He called the wild-eyed man Charlie Crow.

"The old man then told me that he hoped I had brought my poker winnings with me," Carl tells. "He said that Charlie Crow had been mad at me for days for fleecing him."

Carl had no idea what the old man was talking about and told him so. But at the same time, Charlie Crow was descending the stairs, rolling the handle of the knife in his fingers.

"I couldn't move from the spot where I was standing," Carl recalls. "This wild-eyed guy just kept coming down the stairs and I stood there while he walked right up to me and pressed the tip of his knife against my stomach.

"He said, 'It's you I want. It's you I want,' and I could feel the cold tip of that knife easing into my stomach. But then he stepped back."

Carl looked into the man's eyes and told him that he was angry with the wrong man. He could kill him if he wanted, but he was angry with the wrong man.

Charlie Crow's face changed to shock. He walked up to Carl and apologized and tried to hand him the knife.

" 'I want you to gut me,' is what he said," Carl recalls. "He insisted that I take his knife and slice him open so that his insides fell out. He said that he deserved it."

Carl wouldn't take the knife and Charlie Crow grew more frustrated. Then the door opened once again and another man entered the room.

The man resembled Carl Reese to the tee. He and the man who had just entered were identical twins.

The second Carl Reese stayed back by the door.

Charlie Crow then told Carl that the man who just came in was the man he had always wanted, but had killed Carl by mistake. They had looked too much alike.

"I realized then that I had been killed in that place during the Klondike gold rush," Carl said. "This had always been the dark place of my dreams and I had come back to learn that I had been killed by mistake. I had never wanted to die and had never wanted to leave Alaska. Charlie Crow had wanted to kill my twin brother, but had killed me instead."

Carl told Charlie Crow that nobody had to die. He took the knife and tossed it into a corner. Charlie Crow laid down in a fetal position and began to sob.

The twin now began to walk over from the door.

As the twin grew ever closer, Carl came to another shocking realization: the man was his camping partner, Bob. Though they looked identical, he could feel that the man was Bob, who had been his twin brother during the Klondike gold rush.

"Bob looked just like me," Carl tells. "Just exactly. And what was even stranger, when we looked into a mirror over a makeshift bar, we both looked like someone other than ourselves. Bob and I both looked exactly alike outside the mirror—just like me. And inside the mirror, we looked exactly alike as well—but we had different features and even different hair color. We looked like we had when we had lived during the gold rush."

Bob told Carl that he wanted to leave the Midnight Sun right away, and Carl agreed. They stepped out into the snow and after walking a few steps, Bob told Carl that he had done a very foolish thing.

"I was angered by the remark," Carl says. "I tried to tell him that I had saved both our lives, and he kept asking me how. When I told him that we might have both been knifed, he just said that I really needed to get some rest."

It was then that Carl realized that Bob no longer resembled him in appearance. He looked like the Bob he ordinarily knew.

Then Sally was suddenly there, holding him, crying, and he realized further that wherever he had been before, he was no longer there.

But he had been there, in that cabin, with all those people—and Bob, who had once been his brother.

He wanted to turn around and look for the cabin, the Midnight Sun, but no one would hear of it. Back in camp, they served him hot chocolate and made him promise, under threat of being tied down, that he wouldn't leave the tent.

"The strange thing is," Carl says with a smile, "I thought I could smell that honey and whiskey on my breath."

Carl and Sally returned to Alaska late that summer, but try as they might, they never found the two-story cabin below

Chilkoot Pass, on the trail to Dyea. The museum curator said that there had been many old cabins in the area at the time and that most of them had fallen down or were dismantled for firewood.

Bob and LeAnn decided that they would ease off the friendship with Carl and Sally. The night of the incident, Carl realized there was no point in telling Bob his story.

After a while, though, Sally came to wonder if Carl's experience hadn't somehow been real. She had to admit that something had taken place, since Carl never experienced another snow dream after that, and his risk-taking behavior nearly disappeared altogether.

"I'll never totally stop wanting a thrill of some kind," Carl confesses. "But I don't do the crazy things I used to, that's for sure."

And today Carl Reese collects all the books he can about early Alaska and the Klondike in particular, searching meticulously through each one for some mention of a two-story cabin called the Midnight Sun.

The Honeymoon Lodge

I

West Fork Ranch
South Central, Idaho

From the time she first entered school Christy Matthews
knew she was different from most other children. When
she held hands with her friends, she could feel their emo-
tions and know what was happening in their lives. She en-
dured frequent headaches, which were caused by stress,
according to doctors. Yet Christy suffered them even during
her most calm moments.

During a picnic in the third grade, she was playing with
another girl and knew instinctively that her friend would
soon die. When her friend was killed with her parents in
an auto accident the following Monday, she was not only
distraught emotionally, but also terrified at her gift.

For a time, she thought she might have caused it, but

never told anyone. After a number of dreams, during which her deceased friend walked with her along a wonderful river, Christy came to understand that her friend's death had not been her fault.

As she grew older, Christy worked to subdue her abilities until, upon reaching her middle school years, she was almost totally rid of them. Her headaches remained, though, a source of severe irritation and concern.

Then came the late August afternoon in 1994 when she drowned.

She and five other friends, graduated seniors from their local high school, were rafting on the X River. They wanted one last outing before they all went off to separate colleges.

It was late afternoon when the turbulent water capsized their raft. Christy was wearing a life jacket, and she was also a good swimmer, but the initial jolt after being thrown from the raft rendered her helpless.

"It all happened so fast," Christy remembers. "I was knocked unconscious when I went overboard and hit the rocks. I came out of my body and flew over the top of the water, watching myself tumbling. I tried to go down and back to my body. I was scared. Everything went dark, and then suddenly white."

Christy was sitting next to a river, one that was smaller and calmer, with bubbling water. She was wearing her blue graduation gown. The water was a soft blue-green, the trees a deep green, and the sky a mix of blue and turquoise. Birds of all colors flew in all directions and she could hear laughing nearby.

"At first I felt very strange," Christy tells, "and I had no idea at the time why I was wearing the gown. I became more and more used to where I was and I realized that I didn't have the headaches anymore."

The laughing was coming from a congregation of young people her own age. She didn't think she knew any of them, until one got up and walked over to her.

It was her friend who had died in the auto accident.

"Kathy told me I wasn't supposed to be there," Christy recalls. "She was exactly my age but wouldn't tell me how she had grown up. I said that I liked it there and she said, 'No, not yet,' and turned me around. I was angry and turned back around to argue, but I was suddenly tumbling."

Christy awakened on the shore as she was being placed in a body bag. The startled medical technicians stepped back as she began screaming.

"I didn't know where I was or what was happening," Christy tells. "And I hurt all over, so badly that I couldn't bear to move. The pain didn't recede until hours later."

Christy spent weeks in the hospital, going in and out of consciousness, recovering from a broken leg and a broken arm, along with several deep cuts and bruises. During this time she lay wondering at her odd experience. She came to realize that the graduation gown represented not her academic achievements, but the beginning of something spiritually new in her life, something she had already prepared for and was meant to do.

All this understanding disturbed Christy to the extreme and each night while going to sleep, she strived to meet again with Kathy, her childhood friend, on the other side.

Her dreams were not discussions with Kathy, though, but someone else whom she had never met.

Someone who was patiently waiting for her.

Following her near death experience, her gift had returned in full, plus some. For a period of time in the hospital, no matter how hard she had tried, she couldn't suppress it. Nurses who came into the room would start when she told them their troubles.

"It just came out of me," Christy remembers. "I couldn't help it. After a while, when my concussion subsided, I could control myself better. But the nurses had all become wary of me."

She thought often about what had happened that hot August afternoon on the river, but could find no means to explain it. She realized that she had died, and that it had brought up a memory of having died before, as a small child, after having locked herself in an old refrigerator in the garage. Somehow the fridge fell over and the door popped open, freeing her. Somehow, she came to and made it into the house, crying, but everyone thought she had just knocked the refrigerator over, scaring herself.

Now, after this latest incident, she was being forced to try to understand what was happening to her and why. Again, she kept it to herself; she didn't know anyone she trusted enough to discuss it with.

"My parents and my friends were all convinced that I had permanently injured my brain falling from the raft," Christy tells, "but all the medical tests said I had sustained only a mild concussion. They had no idea why I kept going in and out so often. I wasn't injured that badly. After I left the hospital, I went back several times for follow-up tests and everything always checked out fine."

She no longer had her headaches, though, and that made her very happy. She would endure the gift if she didn't have to suffer along with it.

Two years later, during the summer of her second year in college, Christy was working at a bed and breakfast when she came into contact with yet another part of the mysterious unknown—the distant past.

In college Christy had taken a course in the history of the westward migration and when she learned of a job opening at an Idaho ranch that had been there since the gold rush days, she jumped at the chance. Christy went to work at the West Fork Ranch, a noted vacation retreat that catered to a large number of guests each year. The owners, Frank and Sylvia Bottoms, were happy to have her, as Sylvia had an extensive antique collection that Christy could catalogue.

Christy immediately sensed the presence of spirits, both down by the barn and inside the main lodge.

"That didn't seem unusual in itself," Christy recalls. "I've discovered that old buildings and dwellings often have spirits from the past attached to them. They most often stay out of sight, for the most part."

As Christy would soon learn, one particular spirit at the West Fork Ranch was far more restless than the others.

It was during her work with the antiques that Christy discovered a wedding portrait of a young couple, he in a cavalry uniform, she in a long white dress with her veil pulled back.

Christy found the tintype interesting and laid it to one side, to look at from time to time. She thought the young soldier dashing in his uniform, with his heavy dark hair and rugged good looks.

"I actually became enamored of him," Christy admits. "I guess I must have been a sucker for the uniform. Who knows?"

Sylvia Bottoms became aware of Christy's interest in the picture and told her what little of its history she knew. Since most of her collection came with no background information, she found it interesting that Christy had picked that particular portrait from the many others.

"She said she had picked the tintype up at an estate sale and had learned that the couple had supposedly stayed at the ranch with the original owners, as a kind of short honeymoon," Christy recalls. "The soldier and his bride had come out from the East and he was to report to General Oliver O. Howard, to join a force of soldiers being assembled because of Indian problems."

Christy had learned from her college history course that in 1877 some members of the Nez Perce Indian tribe were protesting bad treatment by the white miners and farmers, and were resisting their forced move onto the reservation. No doubt the young cavalryman had become a part of the regiment that was trying to prevent any trouble from starting.

As she studied the picture further, Christy thought that the bride looked familiar, but laughed at herself. There were days when everyone looked familiar, she told herself, even people in a very old picture.

II

The first few weeks went very well for Christy. During the time she wasn't cataloguing antiques, she worked in the kitchen inside the main lodge, and also as one of the caretakers of the Honeymoon Lodge, a large log structure that stood off by itself, with a second-floor landing, complete with table and chairs for relaxing and gazing out at the mountains.

The lodge was usually booked a week at a time, for weeks in advance. But with the coming of a mid-May snowstorm, one of the parties canceled.

"I worked for two days with Sylvia inside the lodge, changing the decor for the couple who was to arrive the following week," Christy recalls. "She had a number of old lanterns and pitchers and vases, and she always kept wedding pictures taken in the 1800s on the wall and the dressers."

Sylvia asked Christy if she thought the tintype of the young soldier and his bride might not look good on the main dresser. Christy agreed, but had a strange feeling in the pit of her stomach.

"I remember at the time that the picture had begun to bother me for some reason," Christy tells. "I didn't know why, but there was something about it. I sensed a deep sadness, then an anger of some kind. It seemed to be attached to the picture somehow."

Christy wanted to watch the sunset that evening but stayed inside because of a sharp wind. That night she dreamed of the bride in the picture, who pulled her veil off and released her long blond hair. Both the dress and the bride's hair were wet, as if she had just come in out of the rain.

Christy sat up in bed, realizing that the same young woman had come to her before, when she lay in the hospital wishing she could again communicate with her dead friend, Kathy. But at the time, the woman had not been wearing a bridal gown, and she hadn't had the determined look on her face. Her hair and clothes had been wet at that time also, making Christy realize for certain that the two women were one and the same.

The following morning Christy ate her breakfast and took a walk beside the river, wondering if her interest in the young soldier had provoked his bride. She returned from her walk to begin the day's work and met up with Sylvia.

"She wanted to know if I felt all right," Christy recalls. "I just told her that I hadn't slept all that well."

She went to work cataloguing antiques but after just a few minutes Sylvia arrived and announced that she needed help in the Honeymoon Lodge.

Christy stood in the doorway while Sylvia walked around the interior, pointing to items here and there that were scattered around the room. It seemed like nearly everything they had meticulously arranged over the previous two days had been moved, even bulky items.

The only thing still in place was the wedding tintype on the main dresser.

"Sylvia thought I had left the window open and that the previous night's wind had blown everything around," Christy says. "I assured her that I hadn't, that I knew the windows had all been closed before I left."

Sylvia shrugged it off and said that it didn't matter. Christy knew from the look on her face that she had some ideas of her own about what might have occurred.

"I asked her if she had ever had this happen before," Christy tells. "She just looked at me kind of funny and said she needed to get down into town and pick up some groceries for the cook."

Christy felt very uneasy being in the room alone. She was aware of someone staring at her, from various vantage points, as if whoever it was would move around, even up into the corners along the ceiling.

"I kept getting this odd feeling, a kind of heat along the back of my neck," Christy tells. "It got pretty intense at times."

Then she appeared.

Christy was hurriedly replacing some old books atop a nightstand when she felt a pressure to turn around. The spirit before her was a young woman near her own age, petite, with long blond hair, drenched with water, that hung down over her shoulders. She hovered above the floor, with no feet beneath her long, dampened wedding gown.

She started to drift forward.

Christy became agitated, asking politely for a respectful distance between them. The spirit became even more intense.

"I wanted to run out of there, but I felt glued to the floor," Christy remembers. "And I wanted to scream, but couldn't. I was too scared to make any noise."

In her mind, Christy asked the spirit what she wanted. The spirit drifted back and withdrew into sparkles of light that soon dissipated. When she could move again, Christy hurried out the door and caught her breath down by the river. Two of the maids were on break, smoking, and one of them said, "You've seen one of the ghosts, haven't you?"

"Which one?" the other one asked.

Without going into detail, Christy said that the Honeymoon Lodge seemed to have some unusual things happening.

"She has too many antiques," one of the maids said. "There's a lot of stuff going on around here."

The maids went back to work and Christy stood and thought about the situation in the Honeymoon Lodge. She liked her job at the ranch and didn't want to risk upsetting Sylvia by leaving the lodge with her job unfinished. She was determined to do her work, disturbed spirit or not.

When she reentered the lodge, she discovered that

nothing was out of place. In fact, something new had been added.

Lying on the dresser, right beside the wedding picture, was a pile of old stationery, together with a quill pen and a jar of ink.

"I knew that Sylvia hadn't put those items there," Christy tells. "And it dawned on me exactly what was happening."

The ink was old and dry, so Christy added a little water and after some work managed to soften it up. With the quill pen and the stationery, she sat down at a nearby table and took a deep breath.

As near as Christy can remember, the letter read:

My dearest Charles,

It is not for me to say how the fates play with our lives. I know you had to do your duty. Please forgive me if I was harsh when you left. I know you didn't wish to cut our time together short. Please allow me to find you, wherever you are, alone or afraid, like me, or lost on that terrible battlefield.

I have remained here by this beautiful river, wishing you might ride back into my life. I hope this letter will find you and bring you back.

I love you, my darling,
Clairissa

When Christy had finished the letter, she realized that it wasn't in her own handwriting. In fact, she didn't even remember writing it.

"I read it and got up and started for the door," Christy recalls. "I then realized that I was walking where the spirit wanted me to, though I can't say whether or not I was possessed by her at the time. I don't think so. I think I was just willing to do her bidding. But only to a point."

Christy arrived at the river and immediately felt a pull toward the water. Even as she approached the banks she realized that she was being forced out into the current.

"I yelled at the spirit to let me go," Christy tells. "I screamed at her. Finally, when I threw the letter into the current, I went back to being myself."

Christy finished her summer at the West Fork Ranch without further incident, due in part, she believes, to the fact that she managed to convince Clairissa's spirit that she had done all she could do. It was up to Clairissa, as Christy tells it, to await Charles's reply to her letter.

"I didn't know what else to do," Christy says. "This woman was determined to have her husband come back to her. She had drowned herself in the river to find him, but when she couldn't she had come back to the lodge. She felt compelled to stay somehow."

In researching the Nez Perce War, Christy discovered that more than one Charles was enlisted in the regiment under General Oliver Howard and that more than one of these men was killed during the battles.

Was it one of those killed at White Bird Canyon, or the Big Hole, or somewhere else along the way during the long and winding march that led from Idaho through

Montana and western Wyoming, and then north to the Canadian line?

She had no way of learning what Charles's last name might be and to try to search would be a waste of time. She would never know where Clairissa's lost love had fallen.

But Clairissa is likely still there, awaiting Charles's answer to her letter, there along the appropriately named Big Lost River of Idaho.

The Mysterious Garden

I

Seaside Point
Portland, Oregon

Six months after her mother's divorce, Amy Ellerman lost her younger brother to a hit-and-run driver. He was skateboarding along a sidewalk near the waterfront when he was struck from behind. Zackery Ellerman died within minutes of reaching the hospital.

Witnesses say that Zack lost control of his board making a turn on the sidewalk and fell sideways into the oncoming vehicle, and that the man seemed unusually composed for someone who had just crashed into a pedestrian. He stared at Zack on the pavement, then returned to his car and sped away, nearly hitting a number of bystanders.

The police later found the car abandoned but the driver was never apprehended.

This was in the early spring of 1988 and Amy was a student at Portland State University. The trauma interrupted her studies so much that she decided not to enroll the next quarter. Instead, she would take some time off from school and stay with her mother, who had taken the loss very hard.

Zack had been a high school freshman, normally outgoing, yet stubborn in a lot of ways. His desire to learn horticulture and rise to the top of the profession astounded everyone. Most young men his age had little or no idea what they wanted to do with their lives.

Over the past three years, Zack and his mother, Eileen, had turned both their front and backyards into a virtual paradise. They had worked together virtually nonstop on the project and had developed a very close bond.

Eileen had entertained visions of a bright future for Zack; his potential had seemed limitless. His uncanny natural knowledge of soils and plants made it simple to introduce new and exotic varieties of flowers and shrubs into the yard. His skills had attracted the attention of serious gardeners.

Zack's favorite spot to work and experiment was located in the northwest corner of the backyard, just adjacent to the vegetable garden. It was here that Zack had planted a variety of bulbs and perennial flowers, the showpiece of the entire landscape.

"He was very protective of the area," Amy remembers. "Almost in a strange way. He didn't want anyone stepping in certain places and he definitely didn't want anyone there without his being present."

Amy had always thought her brother to be somewhat eccentric, and after the divorce, in the last few months prior to his death, he had developed some very strange behavioral patterns.

"He would sit cross-legged in the garden and make odd movements with his hands," Amy remembers. "At first I thought he had decided to meditate there, or something, but that wasn't like him. And the gestures weren't slow or deliberate, but quick and often accompanied by loud noises."

In addition, he often enjoyed sitting by himself in the garden late at night. Though none of the gestures or sounds happened at that time, he still acted peculiar, smearing himself with soil and plant material. And though neither Amy nor her mother ever caught him with alcohol or drugs, he always seemed high on something.

He repeatedly explained it away by saying that he was in sync with his plants night and day, and enjoyed them even in the darkness.

Shortly after Zack's death, interesting things began to happen in his flower garden, as well as the vegetable garden next to it.

While Zack's flowers continued to flourish, the vegetables began to wither and die.

And there was evidence that Zack had never left the yard.

"It actually looked as if someone were actively working the area," Amy remembers. "The soil would be tilled and flower bulbs moved around. I knew Mother wasn't doing it. She was too depressed to do anything in the yard. In fact, she seemed oblivious to the whole thing."

Amy wouldn't allow herself to think that, somehow, her brother was still tending his garden.

But after a period of time, she realized it had to be true.

The first event occurred just after a late-afternoon rainstorm, as the sun began to fall below the horizon. Amy sat on the deck watching birds eat at the feeder before going to roost. She had tried in vain to get her mother to join her, but had then decided to try to relax by herself with a cup of coffee.

While she wondered how to approach her mother a strange thing happened. She was sitting on the deck, selecting courses she would be taking when fall arrived, when she noticed something odd.

"There was a rock pathway that led past Zack's garden," Amy remembers. "Water from a predawn rain had collected near the walkway and I heard the splashing sound of someone's footsteps. I thought a meter reader had come into the yard, but it was too late in the day, and besides that, our cat was hunched down, hissing. I stood up and distinctly saw footprints in the fresh mud along the walkway, as if someone had just gone by and left boot marks behind."

Amy's cat slinked into the house, its tail bristled up like a bottlebrush. Amy thought about getting up and investigating, but she was too frightened. In fact, she was shaking.

After going back inside to fill her coffee cup, Amy returned to the deck and stared out toward her brother's garden. She had certainly heard something, but she didn't want to admit it.

Finally, she got up enough courage to go down to the garden to investigate.

"Every fiber of my being was tingling," Amy remembers. "I knew on some level that Zack was still around and that he had just passed by, but I didn't want to believe it. When I was small we lived in a house that had a ghost, but when it's your brother, that's hard to deal with."

Amy investigated the walkway and discovered fresh tracks. There was an opening in the trees and she could see clearly that the mud in the water hadn't even settled yet. Determined to prove to herself that she wasn't falling victim to grief like her mother, she made her way to the garden shed.

"Mother had arranged all of Zack's rakes and other tools neatly just the night before," Amy recalls. "I had been with her when she did it, trying to get her to talk to me. So I took the key and opened the shed door and almost fainted."

All of Zack's tools were in disarray, scattered here and there, fallen down. And his gardening boots, which his mother had cleaned and set neatly off to one side, were sitting in the middle of the shed, covered with mud and water.

Amy returned to the house and sat inside at the kitchen table, trembling. Her mother had gone to bed early, without even eating. The cat was nowhere to be seen.

As she drank coffee, she began reflecting on how their

family dynamics had drastically changed in less than a year. The months leading up to the divorce had been very draining, filled with tension. After her father's departure, both Zack and her mother had retreated into their gardening.

And now, after Zack's death, it seemed that her mother was spiraling deeper and deeper into depression.

"I was really trying to devise a way to get her out of her funk," Amy recalls. "I realized she needed a lot of time to mourn Zack—as I did, myself. But I thought she was going too far, and I had begun to seriously worry about her."

Amy watched Zack's garden over the following week, knowing someone was there, someone that she couldn't see, but could definitely feel.

"I just knew that sooner or later he would appear in his garden," Amy says, "that I would see him standing there. But I didn't know what to do about it."

Her mother spent a lot of time lying on the couch or in her bedroom. Amy had to constantly open the drapes to allow sunshine into the room, something that had never been a problem before.

Eileen couldn't afford to keep it up much longer. She was rapidly using up all her sick leave and vacation time from her job with the U.S. Postal Service.

Amy considered contacting professional help, but the evening that she suggested it, her mother behaved in a very uncharacteristic manner.

The normally mild-mannered woman flew into a rage.

Amy remembers it vividly, as if she were reliving it.

"She stood up from the table and dumped her plate of spaghetti all over the floor, then threw the plate at me and, luckily, I ducked. It flew into the kitchen and smashed the coffeemaker, and also broke other cups and dishes in the kitchen. I just couldn't believe she did that."

Eileen left the kitchen, headed for the car. Amy tried to stop her but Eileen seemed to have a strength that was also uncharacteristic. She pushed her daughter to the floor and stormed outside.

"I watched her climb into the car and just sit there," Amy tells. "She sat and stared for the longest time, then got out and went into the yard. She walked over to Zack's garden and sat down in the middle of the flowers, smashing some of them. I just didn't know what to do. My father was working for an oil company overseas and hadn't even bothered to return for the funeral, so how was I going to turn to him?"

On that strange evening, Amy stood in the doorway to the deck and watched her mother cover herself all over with damp soil, from head to foot, even smearing it on her face, then smile broadly.

In Amy's mind there were two choices: find help for her mother immediately, or watch helplessly while she slipped into complete insanity.

II

As spring turned to summer, Eileen Ellerman seemed to be content, just as long as she spent a good deal of time in Zack's garden. She placed a shrine to him there, a small table covered with pictures and mementoes of her son's life, which she covered with a thin tarp every morning before she went to work and then again every evening just before retiring for the night.

Amy was glad that her mother had found a way to cope with Zack's loss, including living an ordinary life and getting herself to work each morning, but she didn't appreciate being ignored.

"She ignored me," Amy recalls. "She would walk right past me on her way to the garden without a word. She fixed her own meals and spent every waking hour in that garden. I even saw her talking loudly to herself on numerous occasions, while she moved flowers around and planted new ones. She went so far as to neglect the rest of the yard for the sake of Zack's space."

Suddenly, Eileen Ellerman's condition worsened again. By the end of July she had grown deeply morose and unbearably irritable. Some days she refused to get out of bed and the days she did, she walked around in a stupor.

At the same time, Amy's nights suddenly because extremely draining. Though she hadn't seen him before, Zack suddenly appeared in her dreams nearly every night. She would see him standing in the yard, his face smashed in on one side and his body bloodied from the accident. At times he would be pacing, telling her something that she couldn't hear.

The dreams lessened in intensity when Amy herself began working in Zack's garden. Though she hadn't done a lot of gardening before, she began digging and poking through the soil, just to get some mental relief.

"It's hard to describe," Amy explains. "He became kind of forceful in the last weeks just before he died and in the dreams I got the impression that he didn't like the way things were going, or not going, in his garden."

One day Amy became very concerned when she was working in the garden and her mother came home, rushed from her vehicle, and set upon Amy, pulling her away from the plot.

"She screamed at me to stay out of the flowers and quit ruining Zack's work," Amy recalls. "At first I didn't hear her say 'Zack's work,' and I flew into a rage myself. I'd had it by then and we got into a real wrangle."

The argument nearly turned physical. Eileen picked up a hoe and brought it back before shaking her head and dropping it.

"For the first time since Zack died, she realized that she had gone over the deep end," Amy tells. "She fell to her knees, sobbing. We both sobbed and held each other."

When they had both regained their composure, Amy realized that her mother had said that Zack had been doing the work in the garden, and she began to wonder.

"I realized then that Zack had somehow taken control of me," Amy recalls. "It scared me and I didn't know how to handle it. I was being possessed, it seemed to me, by my brother."

Amy and her mother sought counseling but could get no satisfaction. Over the course of four weeks, they visited three different professionals, each of whom prescribed prescription medicine and rest. There was no resolution to the real issues.

And at the same time, her mother was digressing back into anger and deep depression.

As autumn approached, Amy fought the dreams that came nightly, lighting candles in her room, visiting a local minister, and finally beginning to systematically dismantle the shrine to her brother. She began taking items one or two at a time back into the house. This caused the dreams to escalate and there were times when she saw Zack and her mother, standing together, looking over the garden— and a third figure in the shadows, beckoning the two of them over.

It was the third figure that set Amy to wondering.

The figure was dark and sinister, no one she had ever met. Often the figure would hover off the ground, and her dream would turn completely black. She often awakened to the stench of rotten flesh or vegetables, which even the candles couldn't eradicate.

One evening as a dream of that sort came to her, so vivid and real, Amy got up and went to her mother's room.

But she wasn't there.

Amy took a flashlight and walked out on the deck. At first she couldn't see anything; but as she shined her light toward the garden, she saw a form lying among the flowers.

"I called my mother's name a couple of times, but the figure didn't move," Amy remembers. "So I walked out there, shaking so badly that I nearly fell down."

Amy discovered her mother, fast asleep, holding a shovel tightly in her hands.

She shook her repeatedly and finally got her to sit up.

"She couldn't talk coherently and I knew she had taken sleeping pills," Amy tells. "So I forced her up and made her walk around and then called an ambulance."

Had Amy not found her, a doctor told her later, Eileen Ellerman would likely have died in her son's garden.

In the emergency room, Amy reflected on the dream that had awakened her in terror. She had seen her mother, resting pleasantly, smiling even, as she lay in a grave that had been dug in the middle of Zack's garden. Both Zack and the dark figure had been shoveling soil into the grave.

Over the next week, Amy began watching her mother more closely, and set about to take the shrine down entirely. Her action prompted more bad dreams and more tension between her and her mother.

"But there was no way I could back off from what I was doing," Amy said. "I had to see the thing through."

Amy realized that some force was at work that extended well beyond her brother's spirit wanting her mother with

MIDNIGHT SUN and Other Stories of the Unexplained

him. The third figure, something evil that had been working behind the scenes, was now starting to show itself to her in her room at night.

"I would smell the dead smell and whatever it was would stand in the corner of my room and hiss at me," Amy recalls. "It looked like a blob of black charcoal. I did a lot of praying and that seemed to help. But I knew it wasn't going to go away."

Her problems were compounded by the fact that it was nearly time to begin classes again and there seemed to be no way to start school under the present circumstances.

But Amy didn't want to put off her education any longer and resolved to understand what was happening.

She began by confronting her mother.

"I told her that I was taking her to a doctor and that she had no choice in the matter," Amy remembers. "At first she was going to argue, then she broke down in tears."

After a long discussion, Amy learned from her mother that she, too, had been dreaming of Zack nearly every night and that his spirit seemed to be calling for her to join him.

Amy brought up the third dark figure that had been showing up also, and her mother asked her what it looked like. When Amy described the entity, her mother led her into Zack's bedroom.

What she saw there still scares her.

"She opened the door to Zack's clothes closet and showed me a notebook with strange figures drawn on the cover. One of them was a black figure with strange eyes. It gave me the chills. The book seemed to have a life of its own. I didn't ever want to touch it again."

Amy learned that Zack had put the notebook together over a period of time, collecting bits of information off the Internet and putting it into a prearranged order. And her mother had known about it all along.

"Mother told me that Zack had taken some kind of oath to remain with his garden forever," Amy tells. "He had wanted her to take the oath with him and she had gotten partway through it before deciding it was nonsense and had left the room laughing."

Apparently the oath hadn't been nonsense. But where Zack got the idea to do it seemed a mystery.

Until Amy watched a television program that dealt with demonology.

She learned that the realms of darkness do exist and are part of the troubles that young people face on a daily basis, once they allow themselves to experiment.

"I knew right then that Zack, either alone or with some of his friends, had gotten himself into a bad situation and that this black figure I had been seeing had come to do evil."

While her mother was at work, Amy took it upon herself to end it, once and for all. She took a shovel and, with an incredible amount of will and fortitude, succeeded in digging a deep hole in her dead brother's garden. She heaped everything from the shrine into it and also placed the notebook, which made her sick and dizzy when she carried it, onto the top of the pile.

"I was so intent on finishing it that I just plowed ahead, not caring what else was going on around me," she says. "I wanted to destroy everything that had anything to do with Zack or his notebook. I cried like a baby the whole time."

Amy Ellerman succeeded in her mission to rid her mother and herself of the endless dreams and terror. She turned the lawn mower over and poured gasoline into the hole, then lit a match.

"It exploded like a bomb in my head," Amy remembers. "It burned with an eerie orange glow and then turned sooty black. I thought sure the neighbors and the fire department would show up but everyone in the neighborhood seemed oblivious to it all. I felt like I was inside of a dream, or another world."

Her mother returned from work that evening, feeling rested and content. Her mother seemed to have lost any memory of the past few months, so Amy didn't tell her mother anything about what she had done, only that she had been grieving so deeply that she had forgotten her own identity.

To this day, Eileen Ellerman doesn't know what happened. Amy is married and a professional in the world of Internet technology, and often contributes to Web sites that discourage involvement in occult and demonic activity.

To her dismay, though, the spirit of her brother, Zack, still remains in the yard where she once lived. Despite her efforts to get him help, including a session with a psychic, there seems to be no way to put him to rest.

"He can't seem to break past the idea that he doesn't have to stay at his garden any longer, that the oath was evil and not real," Amy says. "My mother sold the house and I moved away with my husband and as far as I know, Zack is still working with his flowers."

PART TWO

PART TWO

The Dark Angel of Texas

I

El Paso, Texas

Among the killers that roamed the early West, none was more frightening or foreboding than John Wesley Hardin. Depending on the accounts, during the course of his life, Hardin is said to have shot and killed between twenty and fifty men, many of them in cold blood.

And there are those who say, including himself in his own autobiography, that he never killed anyone but in self-defense.

No matter the reasons for his body count, John Wesley Hardin lived a violent life and died in the same fashion. On a hot August afternoon in 1895, Constable John Selmen of El Paso sought him out and shot him in the back of the head with a revolver.

Writer Leon Metz, a respected historian and biographer

of numerous outlaws and lawmen alike, has felt his fair share of negativity while pursuing the lives of these violent men, but nothing could compare to the extreme horror that enveloped him during his research of John Wesley Hardin.

"The story of John Selmen, who killed Hardin, was my first book and it took a heavy toll on me," Leon remembers. "Others, including Pat Garrett, who shot Billy the Kid, were very difficult as well. But when I was done, I put them aside and moved on. John Wesley Hardin is still with me."

Over the years, Metz has taken any number of people to Hardin's grave site, but had never developed an interest in writing about the outlaw. Then in 1993, with readers of outlaw lore looking toward the hundredth anniversary of Hardin's death, Leon suddenly grew interested in profiling the legendary killer.

"If I had even remotely envisioned what I was about to go through," Leon says, "I would have stayed as far away from that story as possible."

Leon Metz doesn't smoke or drink coffee or tea, and he consumes alcohol only on rare occasions, but 'never while at work. However, he does drink sodas to get his mental motors going and wonders if the combination of the caffeine and a building anxiety over the man he was writing about didn't provide a platform for the horror that, for a long period of time, covered him like a heavy, netlike shroud.

"I was halfway through the manuscript when I realized

that I couldn't complete the work by the hundredth anniversary," Leon tells. "It wasn't coming together right."

Comparing Hardin's own words, as he had portrayed himself in his autobiography, with the official record presented problems immediately. Hardin's account was straightforward, but rarely accurate, a combination of self-serving, evasive, and haughty prose that was intended to leave the reader believing that the outlaw was a hero.

"The Hardin I uncovered was far from a hero," Leon recounts. "So I began my portrayal of the man based on official records, contemporary narratives of the time, newspaper stories, and even his own letters. The Hardin I uncovered was far different from the Hardin of his own self-made image."

Determined to tell as closely as possible the real story of John Wesley Hardin, Leon Metz set to work.

And that's when the major problems began.

"We seemed to be mentally communicating," Leon remembers. "And he wasn't happy at all. My writing about him was like slogging through a dark swamp of evil."

Leon never told anyone about it, but kept the strange terrible foreboding feeling that he was being stalked to himself.

Before long, Leon Metz knew with certainty that John Wesley Hardin wanted to kill him.

He told his publisher that he wanted to call his book *Dark Angel*, and subtitle it *The Story of John Wesley Hardin*. His publisher wondered if that didn't sound too much like fiction.

Leon argued that *Dark Angel* fit Hardin to a tee: a

charming, interesting, and gregarious man who would sing and dance and laugh and help you in any way that he could, but with a dark and violent nature that could change the man into the devil himself.

As soon as he began writing about Hardin, Leon Metz fell under full frontal attack.

"One night I shut down the computer after working late and sank into bed," Leon remembers. "When I closed my eyes, my brain suddenly felt as if it were rolling around in my head. There was no pain and no voices, nothing like that. I sat up in bed and touched my right cheek. I thought my brain was literally going to roll out into my hand."

Not wishing to disturb his wife, Cheryl, Leon left the bed to read a magazine and file some papers in the den.

"As long as I focused and stayed active, my brain seemed normal," Leon says. "But as soon as I would close my eyes, my brain would start to roll."

Finally, at 3 A.M., he felt well enough to return to bed.

The weeks went by and the pressure grew ever greater. During a research trip to a town in the Texas hill country, he felt literally engulfed in evil, so surrounded by forces he couldn't explain that he walked the streets for hours. Shortly thereafter, he arrived for a speaking engagement in Sierra Vista, Arizona, and was again overcome with the strange darkness, so much so that he collapsed on a street corner in tears and seriously considered calling home.

"I finally pulled myself together and drove on to the hotel," Leon says. "I made the speech and immediately drove back home, wondering if I wasn't having panic attacks. I hoped against hope that it was an affliction totally unrelated to Hardin."

Then something occurred that made him realize that his affliction had to be caused by the gunfighter himself.

With the hundredth anniversary of Hardin's death, El Paso, Texas, was filled with onlookers taking tours, listening to speeches, and watching intently as a reenactment of the gunfighter's death took place. At 11 P.M. everyone gathered at Hardin's gravesite and tipped champagne to the outlaw's memory.

Joining Leon as an expert on Hardin's life was a psychiatrist from Chicago, Dr. Richard Marohn, a specialist in youth homicidal behavior, who gave lectures and slide shows regarding Hardin and men like him who murdered and couldn't quit. Marohn had a collection of Hardin memorabilia worth over a million dollars and a book of his own that detailed the outlaw's bloody and sordid career.

"He was a big, hale, hearty guy, about five years younger than I," Leon remembers. "We discussed Hardin, but I didn't mention my side effects, and neither did he. I wondered at the time, though."

After the conference, Dr. Richard Marohn returned to his home in Chicago. Two weeks later he was dead.

"By some accounts a stroke, by others, encephalitis," Leon says. "That means the mosquito would have had to have bitten him while he was here in El Paso. I don't care what the record shows, I know that Hardin somehow got him, the same as he was after me."

||

Leon pursued his story even further, digging up more facts, gathering more evidence, proving that John Wesley Hardin had grown used to killing and terrifying anyone who got in his way. The research showed that the gunman drank heavily and cared little for anyone but himself.

Then the horsemen came—faceless, up from the depths of hell.

"They showed up nearly every night, silent, unmoving, mounted men, sitting rock-still in formation," Leon remembers. "I could smell the pungent brimstone odor and through intermittent glimpses of light I could see their horses, hear an occasional snort, and notice a leg quiver. And I could feel Hardin with them, but he never spoke."

Night after night Leon rose in bed, drenched in sweat, shaking violently, calmed only by his wife who insisted that he consult a doctor.

"I told him that I was either dying or going crazy," Leon says. "I thought I would surely run off a cliff."

Finding no physical problems, the doctor prescribed tranquilizers. The dreams receded but the trembling grew worse, accompanied by false feelings of heat and fever. Each time Leon checked, the thermometer registered normal. One night he shook so violently that his wife had to lie across him to keep him in bed.

Even a change of medication did little good. It brought on alternating chills and fever. He avoided the cold as much as possible, hoping to avoid panic attacks. After a time, he had trouble differentiating between what was serious and what was inconsequential.

Through it all Leon Metz finished his book. *John Wesley Hardin: Dark Angel of Texas* won the 1996 Spur Award for biography, presented to him by the Western Writers of America during their convention in Cheyenne, Wyoming. The presenter commented to him that in reading the book, she couldn't tell if he liked or disliked the gunfighter.

"I had no time to respond to that right then," Leon says. "So I made my acceptance speech and sat down."

Today, Leon Metz lives on the edge, waiting for the gunfighter to return, taking low doses of tranquilizers to keep the visions of hell at bay. He no longer drinks caffeinated colas and he's joined a behavioral group in El Paso.

Days and weeks can go by with no problems, but even a little thing can trigger anxiety. If he ever stops the tranquilizers, the odds are great that his horrifying nights will return. He wants no more of John Wesley Hardin's life, but believes that somehow he has become trapped within that strange man's afterlife.

He says that he will always write, but that at least for the time being, he will forgo the subject of gunfighters.

The Valley of Witches

I

Ideal Road
Southwestern Colorado

Just east of Walsenburg, between the Santa Clara and Unfug
Ridges, lies a small valley known locally for its strange history. At the center of everyone's fears are the ruins of an
old cabin that hold many untold secrets.

No one feels at ease here, and most everyone remains
a good distance away when the sun goes down.

However, Paul Wilson of Denver, Colorado, is not one
of those people.

As an archaeologist and adventurer, Paul is drawn to the
unusual; and the Valley of Witches, at one time, lay directly
in the backyard of his father-in-law's ranch.

"My father-in-law thought the stories interesting, but
little else," Paul says. "But my brother-in-law told me he

didn't like the area, and avoided going there, even after lost cattle, if he could. The mystery of the area was just too much for me to ignore."

Stories of unexplained lights and sounds had become part of the local folklore, along with accounts of lost treasure and gold.

"Treasure and gold stories are common," Paul says. "You have to take them with a grain of salt. But there's always a possibility . . ."

In the early 1980s, over a two-year period, Paul and several of his associates combed the area with electronic equipment, hoping to locate something of value. Nothing was found.

"Like I said," Paul says, laughing, "you have to check things out."

Since the daylight hours had proven fruitless financially, Paul decided to investigate the area after sundown, to see what he could discover, but couldn't get any family members to accompany him. Finally, with two close friends, he decided to camp near the cabin ruins and see what developed.

"We camped there a number of nights and nothing at all happened," Paul tells. "I wasn't sure what all the fuss was about. But stories there are, both from today and the past, and some of them are certainly strange."

The strange stories centered around a mysterious old man named Johnson, thought to be an ex-slave, who settled in the area in the 1870s. He kept to himself and stayed away from town, where he realized very quickly that he was not welcome. He acquired food and the goods he needed from passersby on the Ideal Road, once the Old Spanish Trail, or from citizens of La Plaza de los Leones, later Walsenburg.

He always paid for his goods with raw gold.

Soon many of the townspeople began bringing out goods to exchange for his gold, and to hear his incredible violin music. Incredibly talented, he could play waltzes, French reels, and any number of the classics, all flawlessly. In addition, he spoke fluent English, German, Italian, and Spanish, as well as possessing an aptitude for gourmet cooking. He quickly gained a reputation for treating his visitors to great meals and music, with a broad smile and an infectious laugh. But such a man was distinctly out of place in a territory fraught with danger and hard times.

"Pretty soon everyone was leery of him," Paul Wilson says, "even those who came to enjoy his music."

But he did have one friend. John Story, a well-known pioneer of the region, maintained that Johnson would never harm anyone, that he was a gentle soul dedicated to his music and his love of friendship.

But no one else in the area at that time—Mexican, Italian, Austrian, Slavic, and German miners, mostly—could believe a black man could come by so many talents naturally. He had to be acquiring them from an unearthly source.

The mountainous area around the Valley of Witches was rampant with stories of Little People, often referred to locally as Wee Ones, Leprechauns, Trolls, or Tommyknockers, desperately feared by the miners, who spent much of their lives underground. It was said that the reclusive black man was in league with these little beings, who loved to dance to music of any kind.

Perhaps it was the Little People who supplied Johnson with gold, in exchange for his wonderful music. Perhaps it was these same little beings who stole unusual food and spices from passing caravans and traded it to Johnson, allowing him to cook such delicious fare.

After all, the Little People stole everything—including children—from everyone, plus ruining crops and causing accidents and sickness and death, at their will.

No one wanted a man in league with the Little People anywhere near them, especially an ex-slave who shouldn't have those kinds of special talents.

II

Johnson's situation became worse in the summer of 1880 when three women arrived in La Veta. They are said to have been footloose and of suspicious nature: one a Mexican, another a French gypsy, and the third a mixture of races.

Upon their arrival, they were immediately shunned, and their credibility suffered even more when it was learned they had driven their wagon to Johnson's cabin.

Before long, a group of people banded together to drive

the women from the area, based largely on the testimony of a local who insisted that he had witnessed the three women dancing around a fire with the Little People, accompanied by Johnson on his fiddle.

When questioned, the women insisted that he had merely helped them gather wild mushrooms, nothing else. Their story was not believed and they were asked to leave, or suffer the consequences.

Now John Story was cornered and questioned again. Of course he knew of the Little People living in the nearby Spanish Peaks area, and the stories told by trappers and Indians, who said only that they were gentle mountain spirits who wished only to be left alone.

In 1983, Paul Wilson and two associates were doing geological field research when their four-wheel drive became hopelessly stuck in a sandy wash. As they began their trip out, they discovered they were walking on the bed of the old Ideal Road.

Paul had just begun the story about Johnson when one of his associates stopped and said that he heard something. "At first, I didn't hear anything," Paul remembers, "but then I heard it as well. We all three heard it distinctly." The faint sound of violin music.

A short ways farther, around a small bend, they saw a greenish yellow light hovering about five feet above the ground.

"I've seen swamp and mine gas many times before,"

Paul relates. "It wasn't either of those. The light was much brighter and its shape was well defined, human in proportion."

The closer they got to the light, the clearer the music became.

Paul wondered at not only what he was hearing, but how he was hearing it.

"The sounds were all around us, not just coming from the light itself," he says. "An incredibly beautiful piece, that seemed to resonate clear through us."

Paul's two associates grew nervous and became anxious to leave.

"I tried to calm them while listening at the same time," Paul remembers. "I believe it was a waltz, but I've never heard the tune before or since."

Suddenly one of Paul's friends began shouting, insisting that they leave before something happened to them. The light immediately went out and the music faded like a distant echo.

While continuing their walk, the three discussed their unusual experience. It had truly taken place and Paul wondered if they had somehow interrupted what he terms "a private concert, a display of love simply for the music, held by the single performer played solely for God and the wonder of nature."

Paul Wilson never learned what happened to the mysterious man named Johnson, when or how he died. Perhaps he was killed, or he might have died naturally, no one can say.

It is an evening that will always remain with Paul Wilson and his two friends, a haunting reminder of the past that harbored no ill will, simply an act of generous hospitality displayed by a simple man with an incredible gift.

"I've debated going back, but haven't," Paul says. "Perhaps it was a once in a lifetime experience."

And, as Paul explained it, the old man must have his reasons for staying and playing the violin in the soft night air. It was his pleasure, in life and now in death, to entertain people the best way he knew how.

Dark and mysterious, the crow is a symbol of the
unexplained, a keeper of secrets, a courier along
the pathway into the spirit world.

(Light Sculpt Designs)

Calamity Jane, as she appeared in her heyday.
Was she the "Shadow in the Park"?

(Adams Museum, Deadwood, South Dakota)

Joyce Thierer, who portrays Calamity Jane.

(Joyce Thierer)

Ghostly mist, a common occurrence
where the dead are gathered.

(Light Sculpt Designs)

Many believe that the round orbs that float in
cemeteries are souls of the departed,
wandering, waiting to move on.

(Don Peterson)

Houses with strange and unusual happenings
often have an eerie mist surrounding them.

(Scott Thon)

When is an owl an owl, and when is it a shape-shifter?
A question to ponder in the Southwest desert country.

(Light Sculpt Designs)

John Wesley Hardin, the Dark Angel of Death.

(Leon Metz)

The Shadow in the Park

I

Coffeeville, Kansas

The West is filled with fairs and rodeos and horse races, events that bring back the old days, the times when the land was open and wild. Dalton Days takes place every fall in the little town of Coffeeville, Kansas, and draws tourists and historical reenactors alike from all over the country.

To the reenactor and historical performer, these functions provide the best platform to live out the times of a bygone era, to re-create the past as close as possible to the real thing.

Joyce Thierer has been working as a historical performer, in the Chautaqua style, for over a decade and does the likeness of Martha Jane Cannary, better known as Calamity Jane, to a tee, right down to tipping her hat to the crowd. She has portrayed the unusual woman over six hundred times since first beginning, gaining her knowledge through a great deal of research and long hours of practice, training herself to become the character that was Calamity Jane.

"Some have labeled me a method actor who looks like Jane, with a historian's mind," Joyce relates. "She was a very strong woman for her time and did a lot of things women weren't supposed to do. She got in trouble for it a good many times, but she just kept on being herself. And now she'll be forever famous."

Calamity Jane is best known for her work as a scout for the U.S. Army during the Indian wars, including a stint with General George Custer in the Black Hills of Dakota Territory, as well as for her relationship with Wild Bill Hickok, the frontiersman and gunfighter who was shot in the back in a saloon in Deadwood, South Dakota, while holding the now-famous Dead Man's Hand of cards—aces and eights.

"That was a particularly hard time for her," Joyce says. "She had come to know Bill very well and to lose a friend like that changed her in many ways. This just added to the string of losses in her life."

It was after Hickok's death that Calamity began drifting around the West, trying her hand at prospecting for gold and driving freight wagons from settlement to settlement, holding her own during one of the western frontier's most dangerous eras.

"I know she has been portrayed as tough and ready for anything," Joyce continues, "but I like to portray her from every aspect that I can, and show her as the complicated but caring woman that she was. I hope I'm doing that."

———

Dalton Days in early October of 1990 was one of Joyce Thierer's first chances to play the role of Calamity Jane in public. The setting was Coffeeville's city park, where a contingent of reenactors dressed as soldiers, fur traders, cowboys, and other frontiersmen and women had set up their tents and outdoor fires to live in the past for the weekend.

"You couldn't enter their camps with foam cups or anything like that," Joyce tells. "Everything had to be authentic, right down to the minutest detail. It was like walking into another time and place, then walking back out again."

The day was filled with activities throughout all of Coffeeville: Bands played everywhere, a craft fair was in full swing, and a carnival operated in one sector. But one of the main attractions was the reenactment stage, where everyone could get a glimpse of a famous outlaw, or lawman, or mountain man, as portrayed by a modern-day individual immersed in a personality from the past.

After numerous characters had come and gone, it was Joyce's turn to take the stage. It was near 7 P.M. and twilight had settled over the gathering. Everyone anxiously awaited her performance, settling into lawn chairs and gathering in tight groups along the sloping hill that formed an amphitheater around the stage.

Joyce threw her saddle over her white saddle rack and nervously began her performance. The streetlights were flickering, not quite on and not entirely off, casting half shadows throughout the park, making it impossible for her to see the spectators clearly.

"I knew they were out there, but I couldn't see their faces," Joyce remembers. "The whole area had taken on a kind of opaqueness. It was like looking at dark water in a plastic jug."

Joyce began falling into Calamity's character, telling stories of the frontier and the part she had played in the history of the Old West, wondering to herself how the audience was accepting her, for the lighting had by now grown even worse.

"Everything was completely dark," she says. "All I could see were some Indians dressed in white skins mixing with the crowd. I could hear people talking and a few laughs; that's the only way I knew anyone was watching."

She became aware of one particular onlooker closer to the stage, the only one she could see fairly clearly. The figure was a small cowhand lying down just beneath her and to the left, hat low, propped up on one elbow, watching her intently, nodding on occasion to segments of her performance.

During one part of the act, Joyce pushed her hat up with her fist, bringing the little cowhand up immediately.

"This person sat bolt upright and glared at me," Joyce remembers. "I saw the cowhand jab his own hat up, showing me that he had used his thumb, not his fist. I was startled, so the next time, I used my thumb and the cowhand nodded in approval and settled back down."

II

When Joyce finished her performance, the applause was overwhelming. She was a hit, one of the best performances of the entire event.

She was flooded with questions. Everyone wanted to know all they could about Calamity Jane and also about Joyce Thierer, the person who had been so convincing as the frontier woman. People were crowding the stage, eager to praise her and give their approval.

Through it all, she searched for the small cowhand, eager to thank him for showing her the correct way to tip her hat. But amid all the commotion, she lost sight of him.

"I searched everywhere in that park," Joyce relates, "but couldn't find hide nor hair of him. I was sorely disappointed."

She continued to talk to her admirers, thanking them for their support. Through it all, the small cowhand remained in the back of her mind.

She looked among the people, hoping he might still show himself.

But it never happened.

Then she began to wonder: Had it actually been a him?

Could it have possibly been a woman, dressed like a man?

Calamity Jane herself had often been mistaken for a man, had more than once been working and living among miners and soldiers before finally being recognized.

So, had the frontier character at the foot of the stage been a man or a woman?

Impossible to tell.

During the drive to her next performance, Joyce thought a lot about her experience. The small cowhand, dressed so authentically, had been equally as vague in the dim light as the other audience members, but somehow had still managed to capture her attention when showing her how to tip her hat.

Yes, how to tip her hat correctly, just as the real Calamity Jane had tipped her own hat, no doubt.

Since that time, Joyce has portrayed the famous frontier woman hundreds of times, realizing each time how complex the real person's life had been.

"I wish to honor her," Joyce says, "to show the real woman and not the one of the mythic West. Of course she told lies about herself, as all the famous westerners did. That was the custom. She was a blend of so many things, a persona that has been added to in layer upon layer upon layer, like a deep road bank layered with many different rock formations."

When Joyce gives her performance it is common to have people come up to her afterward and gaze into her eyes, shake her hand, even clutch her clothing, as if meeting the real Calamity Jane.

"Once my hat is on, Jane comes out," Joyce says. "When the hat comes off, I become the academic I was trained to be, answering questions in a precise way."

Joyce Thierer says she will likely never really know the true identity of that unusual spectator, lost with all the others that night in that Kansas park awash in darkness, lying in the grass beneath the stage, resting on one elbow, hat down low. But that person had certainly made a lasting impression and now during every single performance, Joyce always uses her thumb to tip her hat back.

The Old Man and the Crow

I

Navajo Indian Reservation
Northwestern Arizona

Tom Moran arrived at Arizona State University from his
home in Pennsylvania in the fall of 1989 to begin course
work in the study of archaeology, a profession that had held
his interest since his first trip west as a boy some years before. The idea that he could learn the means by which to
study ancient cultures while actually residing in the lands
they once lived in seemed too good to be true.

By the spring of his sophomore year, Tom's major
source of information had been textbooks and classroom
lectures. His grades were very good and his enthusiasm
high. He had already made some assumptions about the
early people and their lives, and believed that he was on

the road to knowing what the ancient cultures were all about.

He had made a couple of trips with friends into Navajoland, as they called it—areas on the reservation where the people lived simple lives and could be observed in their natural surroundings. On both occasions, Tom and his classmates were met by individuals who warned them soundly against intrusion where they didn't belong.

"At first I didn't take it too seriously," Tom remembers. "I just thought they were angry because of the early days and the way they had been mistreated, and were still being mistreated. I wanted them to know I wasn't someone who didn't respect their culture."

As good as his heart might have been, Tom didn't understand the difference between respect and understanding. He didn't realize that the understanding part was nearly impossible for someone not born into the culture and who wasn't living within its parameters on a daily basis.

In the spring of 1991 Tom and two companions packed enough food and gear for a long weekend and made their way into the heart of the reservation, stopping to look at various ruins sites and taking notes.

Before long, they realized that they weren't welcome there.

"We met a tribal cop who asked us why we were poking around," Tom recalls. "I told him that we had good intentions and just wanted to learn. He studied me and asked me if I really had any idea what I wanted to learn. I said, of course, the Navajo ways and how to preserve them. He said that was all well and good, but that I would need a big stick with a lot of rings on it if I was going to do that."

Tom and his classmates left, unable to understand what they had been told. The following September they returned, this time to a different part of the reservation, in hopes of avoiding the big cop they had met that spring.

They stopped to eat a lunch of sandwiches and chips in the shade when Tom spotted a large stick lying beneath a rabbitbrush plant. He picked it up and studied it, noting that there were concentric rings around the middle that had once been painted in various colors that were now faded.

"I felt very strange holding it," Tom recalls. "It felt alive. The other two looked at me and told me to get rid of it. But I wanted to keep it. It didn't register with any of us at the time that the big cop from the previous summer had warned us about such things."

Tom placed the stick next to his belongings in their vehicle and within minutes they had a visitor.

"There was no cop this time," Tom remembers, "but there was an old Indian man, with pure white hair, who appeared out of nowhere. I assumed that he was Navajo. He was very small, with a battered hat and old clothes. He looked like a sheepherder, possibly, but he wore boots with big silver spurs on them. They even looked old, like Spanish rowels, or something, and they were polished to a bright sheen. He was about thirty yards away, standing still, just staring at us."

Tom's friends said that they should go, but Tom didn't feel like leaving, so he walked toward the old man.

"It didn't seem as if I were gaining any ground," Tom

tells. "I just kept walking and he kept the same distance apart from me, seemingly without moving. I turned around to look at my friends and ask them what was going on. When I turned back around, he was standing right in front of me."

When Tom asked his friends later how the man had done it, they were puzzled by the question. They both said that he had walked right up to the old man, nearly running into him.

"I got over my surprise and asked the man if he could speak English. He shook his head no, then pointed to a crow sitting on a nearby rock that, like the old man, just showed up out of nowhere. It flew over and lit on the old man's shoulder, then talked to me telepathically. It scared me, so I turned and left."

As he walked away, Tom looked back periodically and noticed that the old man had sat down and that the crow was jumping up and down in front of him. The crow was cawing and the old man laughing.

That was disturbing in itself, but what really got to Tom the most was the fact that the crow had asked to see his big stick with the rings around it.

When Tom returned to his friends, he was reluctant to say that the crow had spoken to his mind. Instead, he said that the old man had warned them against being on sacred ground, and that they should leave.

"Looks like he's got that crow pretty well trained," one of Tom's friends commented.

Tom said that it was indeed an unusual crow. Tom took the stick out of the vehicle and, after taking a look at the old man, tossed it back under the rabbitbrush plant. When he turned to look again, the old man was gone.

But there were now two crows where just the one had been.

Tom and his classmates immediately packed up their gear and everyone was happy to go. After that day, they never returned to the reservation.

At least not physically.

II

After graduation, Tom Moran went to work as an archaeologist for a federal agency in Arizona. He found his work to be every bit as rewarding as he had thought he would. The trouble was, in his mind, he had never left the Navajo Reservation.

Darkness of any kind, for Tom Moran, had become a living nightmare.

"I couldn't stop dreaming about that old man and his crow," Tom relates. "They wouldn't leave me alone. I kept finding myself back on that desert with them, holding the stick in my hands, and they would do the strangest things to me."

The first series of dreams involved the old man nodding while the crow spoke. Tom felt frozen, unable to awaken, and unable to take his eyes off the bird.

"That bird would say things and nod at me, things like,

'Pull four blades of grass today and count them every hour on the hour.' If I didn't do it, they would be back that very night and I'd go through the same thing."

In another dream he would be instructed to carry four tiny pebbles around in his mouth all day long. If he didn't comply, the same dream would come to him again that night, and every night thereafter until he did what he was told.

"I could continue to fight it and go crazy," Tom says, "or I could go along with them and feel foolish. I decided to feel foolish over going to the loony bin."

Tom says that over time, the process changed him.

"Crazy as it sounds, I became very much in touch with the earth," he says. "I could feel the grass in my fingers even though I wasn't touching it, and I could feel the rocks, the trees, everything. Birds and animals would stop and I was certain that I saw them smiling. It cost me a marriage, but what choice did I have?"

Tom did what the old man and the crow instructed him and by the summer of 1994 the dreams had ended, he hoped for good.

They were, in fact, only beginning.

On a rainy fall night in 1994, Tom Moran was back in Pennsylvania at his parents' house for a short visit. While the rain beat down on the roof, he lay in deep sleep, watching the crow and the old man walk toward him.

"That's how the nightmares would always begin," Tom

says. "They would come to me and tell me to do some-thing. But this time as they came, the old man was holding a mug of something that he forced down my mouth. I couldn't wake myself and I couldn't yell or scream out loud, only inside my head."

Tom felt himself falling down into a hole, where he passed all kinds of strange places filled with strange beings. He finally stopped and stood in front of what he knew to be a huge kachina, a spirit from deep in Navajo antiquity. The kachina touched him and Tom awakened.

"I didn't know where I was for the longest time," Tom tells. "I sat up in bed and tried to focus my eyes and finally laid back down and saw the room fill with concentric cir-cles, just like the ones on the stick I had found."

After Tom returned to work, the dynamics of his dreams changed once again. For a time the old man would approach holding an ear of corn. The crow would fly circles around Tom, holding him in place while the old man stripped kernels from the ear of corn and tossed them up into the air.

"For weeks in my dreams it would rain corn down on me," Tom recalls. "It wasn't hard like regular corn, but more as if it had been cooked, and it was very hot. Every night I felt a thousand little burning spots all over my body."

As the dreams continued, the old man would throw more corn skyward. Tom was always tempted to look up, but would instead fix his gaze on the old man.

"I knew that if I ever looked up, kernels would drop into both eyes and blind me," Tom says.

Every morning when he awakened he would check himself for burn spots. He would find no marks anywhere on his body—until he looked into the mirror.

"They always showed up in the mirror, but not when I looked directly at my body," Tom remembers. "I was very certain that I was going crazy. Then, when I would take a shower, they would disappear and be gone even when I looked in the mirror."

Finally, the corn dreams ended and he slept well for nearly a month. He thought that he had gotten past his desert terrors, for the old man and the crow never returned.

But he was a changed man, so very changed that he had no means by which to explain it and no one to turn to.

Tom Moran still finds himself changing into something he doesn't want to be.

A crow.

"I will look in the mirror and see a crow's head where mine should be," Tom tells. "If I look farther down my body, I'll see black wings. It happens spontaneously, but it will happen also when I will it. I don't think most people could see it, but I know that if I will that, they would be able to."

Tom again sought counseling. One psychologist told him that Tom had a personal mythology that he had associated with Navajo culture and he needed to concentrate on other things besides archaeology.

"In essence," Tom says, "he thought I was imagining the whole thing."

Another psychologist took an approach closer to what Tom believes to be the truth—that he got involved with something he didn't understand and that the old man, certainly a spirit and shape-shifter, had turned him into a shape-shifter as well.

"He told me that if I truly wanted to be rid of the curse of the old man and the crow," Tom tells, "I would need to go for help to a person that knew the culture, likely a Navajo who knew how to help me."

Tom has since tried to return to the reservation, to see if he can't find someone to help him. But he can't make himself do it for fear of something worse happening. He knows when the episodes come that cause him to change, and he is able to deal with it, even in public, though he has had some strange experiences there as well.

"If it happens in public, children will often see me as a crow, while the adults won't," Tom says. "But every once in a while an adult will be able to see and though it rarely startles them, they try to approach me to learn about me."

Tom is not interested in joining spiritual groups who want to know his story. He wants to be able to work in peace and somehow find a way back to normality.

It won't come easy, or soon, Tom knows. The very culture that could help him wants nothing to do with him.

"Indian people, of all tribes, won't come anywhere near me," Tom laments. "I'm having trouble now in my profession."

Tom Moran says he wants people to know that what happened to him could happen to anyone, and to listen when someone warns you about getting into something you can't ever get out of.

The Large Winged Shadow

I

San Juan Mountains
Northern New Mexico

On the eve of her son's thirteenth birthday, Carmen Garcia
Edmonds allowed her son, Richard, to become the guest
of his maternal uncle, Lucio Garcia, on his first deer hunt
into the mountains. Having grown up in urban Los Angeles,
Richard hadn't learned much of the Indian/Spanish culture
that was Carmen's heritage or the natural ways of the
woods. She thought it would be a good time for him to
start.

Recently divorced, nearly thirty years old, and looking
for meaning in her life, Carmen had brought her son from
the suburbs of Los Angeles to a small town in the desert
outside of Albuquerque, New Mexico, where her parents
and family lived. It was a far cry from the jet-set life she

and Richard had become used to, but Carmen believed that they would be much better off with her relatives than the two of them struggling to find a place to live and a job for her in LA.

"I was an unhappy person and I didn't want that rubbing off on Richard," Carmen remembers. "I believed he could fit in better in a small town with kids who, like him, were living in two different cultures but were getting support from their aunts and uncles and their grandparents on their native and Spanish side. It's hard for a kid like him to adjust to a new life that's not nearly as fancy as the one he had left."

Richard's father was an airplane pilot and Richard knew that his parents had been having trouble for a number of years. He had seen the divorce coming and although he hadn't spent much time with his father over the years, leaving LA was still a shock.

"At first I didn't fit in with the kids from our new town," he says. "I was used to things that they didn't have, like a computer and my own television set. The only way I broke in was that I could play basketball better than most of them."

Though Richard could survive very well in the white world, his grandmother and all his aunts and uncles told him and his mother that he needed to know what it was to be a native person, a person of the land where his ancestors had lived.

"That's why I wanted Richard to spend more time with his uncle, so he could teach him these things," Carmen says. "I thought it was very important."

When Richard left with his uncle to hunt deer, Carmen was happy. But little did she know that, because of her, he would learn a great deal more about a seldom-discussed side of his heritage that neither he nor she had ever imagined.

By the time Richard had been gone with his uncle for five days, Carmen had grown ever more restless and worried that something had happened to them. Richard's uncle had said they would be back at the end of three days, four at the most, and that they would call at least once during that time. By the end of the sixth day, with no word from Richard's uncle, Carmen decided to go looking.

"My relatives all told me to stay home and not to worry about Richard," Carmen remembers. "They said that he was in good hands and that they would return soon. I argued that something must have happened to them and that I wanted to go to the authorities. But they didn't want that and they essentially warned me against going up to look for my son."

Carmen didn't listen, and called the authorities about her son. They told her to wait a few days and call back. Infuriated, she decided to travel into the mountains alone.

"My aunt Lorita was chosen from among the women to deal with me," Carmen recalls. "She took me aside and said that if I wouldn't listen then she could find a means by which I could check up on Richard without going on a long and dangerous chase."

Carmen realized that Lorita was right, that traveling

alone was not a good idea. She did what her aunt requested by gathering together new blankets and a pot for cooking, and some fresh bread to take along, thinking it was for them.

A day passed while she did this and Carmen realized that her aunt was stalling.

Carmen was getting into the car when Lorita stopped her.

"She agreed to go with me," Carmen tells. "She told me to do everything that she said, no questions asked, and that I would learn for myself that Richard was okay. But it wouldn't be a good thing. She was very upset, but she knew that I would go alone if no one came along."

During their trip toward the mountains, Lorita explained to Carmen over and over that no one, especially women, went around alone anywhere in the area at night. Too many strange things happened and no one was safe. Carmen finally realized that she was referring to the age-old fear of *brujos* and *brujas*, the male and female witches that plied their trade in the darkness.

"I told my aunt that I didn't believe any of it," Carmen tells. "I had heard a lot as a young girl, but I had left with my mother when I was just starting school and so I didn't believe everything I'd been told."

Lorita then told her that not all witches were bad, but that she herself knew an old woman who was kind and very helpful. In fact, they were going to meet her. Carmen learned that her aunt had agreed to go along not because there would be strength in numbers, but so she could take her niece to the witch's home. That's what the blankets and food and cooking items were for, as presents.

"She explained to me that this woman could prove to me that Richard was fine and in good hands, and that I would pay her for it. I didn't know what to think, but at that point I didn't feel I had any choice in the matter."

It was well after dark when they arrived at the *bruja's* home, a small, nondescript adobe structure called a hogan, which sat alone where the desert met the foothills of the mountains. At first, Carmen was reluctant to leave the car but her aunt finally convinced her that she had gotten herself into it and, therefore, should complete it, or face endless bad luck for herself and the entire family.

"She told me in so many words that the witch was waiting for us and would do us harm if we backed out," Carmen tells. "I didn't know whether to believe her or not, but I didn't want to be wrong."

II

Richard had been with his uncle for five days and they had yet to get a clear shot at a deer. His uncle blamed it on the heavy hunting in the area, which had reduced the population down to a fraction of what it had once been. But Richard knew that there was more to being out in the woods than merely shooting a deer.

During their time together, Richard and his uncle had gotten to know each other very well. They shared food and camping chores, with Richard getting many lessons on living in the wild. He had come to enjoy his uncle's company and felt good about their long conversations beside the campfire.

Richard soon learned the vast differences between life in the city and finding oneself in the wide-open spaces. It scared him at first, but his uncle soon dispelled any ideas that they would be harmed by predators—from this or any other world.

It was the term "other world" that made Richard begin a series of questions. His uncle showed him a little bag that he always kept in his pants pocket and told him that one day he would have such a bag of his own, or something similar.

"I learned from him about the things that have been carried down over many generations and that still happen," Richard explains. "A lot of people think it's a bunch of hooey, but it isn't. Even some native people are saying this, and it's not good."

Richard's uncle delved deeply into the cultural heritage of his people and insisted that his nephew understand how important it is to believe in the power of good, and that the good he was speaking of was with them in the mountains.

"When I finally got over my worries, I had never felt such peace before," Richard remembers. "The air was fresh and clean and the stars were so bright. It was truly amazing. I had thought at first that I would be considered a failure if I didn't get a deer, but I soon realized that everyone at home thought I would be very lucky if I did."

During this entire time, neither of them gave any thought to Richard's mother, that she might be worrying about them. Then on the last night Richard brought it up and his uncle said they would head for home in the morning.

But it was still a long ways from daylight.

Carmen sat in the old adobe hogan, finally relaxed enough to carry on a conversation. At first she had been petrified, but then realized that the very small woman, mostly Navajo Indian, posed no threat to her.

"I expected her to be mean, with hard eyes and scraggly hair," Carmen remembers. "Instead, she was a very pleasant woman with a nice smile, who made me feel comfortable."

Outside the hogan, to one side of the doorway, a heavy concentration of juniper twigs had been laid out in a large circle, with a collection of stones and rocks inside, arranged into symbols.

By torchlight, Carmen could see that the inside was sparsely furnished, with but a few blankets spread over a large bag filled with grass that the woman used for a bed. There was no plumbing of any kind. Water came from a nearby spring and all the cooking was done outside.

She also noticed a number of clay pots filled with various herbs. Large and small roots alike lay on blankets and atop flat pottery plates both inside and outside.

Carmen drank tea from a bowl and ate a mixture of meat and berries and cornmeal. She still knew her Spanish and had taught Richard to speak it as well, but the *bruja* and her aunt began speaking in Navajo, and after a short time the features on the old woman's face suddenly changed.

"She looked like a different person entirely," Carmen remembers. "She became more masculine and her eyes more intense. I wanted to leave but Lorita said that wasn't possible."

Carmen sat and listened to her aunt and the old woman, having no idea what they were saying. Finally, Lorita told her they would go outside and wait to be joined by the woman.

"Lorita told me not to look into the hogan, so that I wouldn't lay eyes on the witch while she prepared herself for helping me," Carmen recalls. "I once again became frightened, only much worse than before. But I had gotten myself into it."

Carmen faced away from the hogan, peering out into the night. Everything seemed to be moving, every bush and rock alive with some shadow behind it. She asked Lorita if she might be seeing things and her aunt explained that there was no cause for alarm.

The old woman emerged from her dwelling, carrying a small pot of burning herbs and a large bird wing. She chanted while she walked four circles around Carmen, fanning the smoke around with the wing.

When she had finished, she stood in front of Carmen and looked directly into her eyes.

"I was held fast," Carmen relates. "I couldn't move and I couldn't speak, though I wanted to scream. She seemed to be putting herself into me somehow. I could feel it happening and I couldn't stop it."

Carmen discovered herself feeling light and airy. Her aunt helped her down to the ground, where the three of them sat in a triangle, cross-legged near the fire. Carmen's aunt then blindfolded her and told her to just relax while the old woman prayed.

After the *bruja* had finished, Lorita turned Carmen around to face away from the fire. The witch sat down directly behind her, chanting in a low voice, waving the large bird wing. Within moments, Carmen felt her consciousness lifting into the air, soaring through the dark desert sky toward the mountains.

She opened her eyes and knew that she, somehow, was actually soaring above the trees and rocks. She felt she was herself, her own consciousness, but realized also that someone else was acting within her own self, guiding the direction they flew.

"I knew that I was a bird," Carmen tells. "I can't explain how it feels to know you're something other than what you believe yourself to be. I couldn't speak of it for a long time, except among my relatives, but now I know that such things happen to others and that I wasn't going crazy that night. I wanted to see my son and as I flew into a canyon, I saw a campfire with two people sitting beside it. I knew immediately it was Richard and his uncle, sharing stories, having a good time, and that I had nothing to worry about."

With the witch's help, Carmen had indeed found her son and was relieved to learn that he was very much alive and well. But her gladness was short-lived and, as she would later learn, things might have gone very badly for both her and the *bruja* woman.

In her stubbornness to learn about Richard's well-being, Carmen had forced the issue to the point of entering a strange place, and would learn very soon that her actions carried a very heavy price.

III

In her mind, Carmen had felt herself lifting off the ground, flying, seeing her son, and landing back at the fire in but a split second of time. In but a flash she had discovered herself seated beside the fire, with her aunt removing her blindfold. It had all happened so quickly that she wondered if it had merely been a dream.

Perhaps she had been tricked and had paid for nothing, really.

She wanted to ask the witch how she had formulated an image of her son like she had. She wanted to know how it could be real and if the tea itself had been used somehow to manipulate her.

"I started to talk but my aunt covered my mouth," Carmen remembers. "She was very angry. She took me by the shoulders and shook me and asked me if I was satisfied. After thinking a moment, I said that I had seen Richard and that, yes, I was happy. She said that I should leave it at that and that we should go."

On the way home, Lorita asked Carmen if she remembered anything about her experience except that she had seen Richard by the fire with his uncle and realized that all was well. Carmen replied that she remembered only that and nothing more, but she sensed that her aunt was hiding something and pressed her for information. Her aunt then told her that they would discuss it the next day.

In reality, a startling occurrence had happened, and Carmen and the old *bruja* had nearly been killed.

Carmen would realize this when Richard returned from hunting late the following afternoon. He greeted her warmly and said that they hadn't gotten any deer, but that something very strange had occurred the previous night. He and his uncle had been talking when they saw a huge shadow float into the top of a pinyon pine, just above the fire.

"It was an owl, so huge that it seemed impossible," Richard told his mother. "We both stared at it and I became very frightened."

Richard's uncle had decided that such a bird wasn't welcome in their camp. An owl can often bring omens of death, so while Richard crouched near the fire, his uncle picked up his rifle and snapped off a shot. Had he been less nervous, Richard told his mother, he might have hit the bird.

"I saw a twig fly right beneath where the owl was sitting," Richard recalls. "It took off on huge wings. That bird just missed getting killed."

Carmen Garcia Edmonds will never forget that night. She is not allowed to. That is what she believes. Her dreams are often controlled by the small Navajo *bruja* who helped her locate her son. She dreams of flying again and landing in trees and watching people stare at her, people she has never met before, people she will likely never meet.

"I believe the witch is exacting payment from me, for what I put her through," Carmen says. "My aunt gave her the presents, but it was me who caused the problems, is the way it seems."

Carmen has since learned that witchcraft is alive and well in southwest Indian country and that it's nothing to be trifled with. Had she listened to her aunt, she would have had faith that Richard was being watched over by his own protectors and that his time with his uncle was important.

So that she will never forget, as if she could, her aunt is teaching her even more about what goes on. They visited a different kind of witch, a male *brujo*, who had been shot but survived. A bullet had broken his right arm and he can no longer use it. He must rely on others; and even though his relatives know he is a witch, they provide for him.

So with each nightfall, Carmen wonders if the *bruja* will come for her, to take her around the deserts and mountains of New Mexico, leading her into situations that leave her terrified.

For now she has no choice, until her debt is paid, if it ever can be paid.

PART THREE

The Dark Game

I

Graham, Texas

It is a common occurrence among young people, especially, to be curious about games that put them in touch with the paranormal. Though the games are seemingly harmless, nothing could be further from the truth.

Jimmy Lowery, now the Reverend Dr. Jimmy Lowery, of Carrolton, Alabama, spent autumn 1996 in Graham, Texas, where he and his now ex-wife, together with their children, survived a harrowing experience with the dark side. It was an event that he will never forget.

"We had just moved into an older house," Jimmy recalls. "We had a few months until we were to move back to Alabama. Little did I know what was going on in that house at the time, and I can't imagine what might have gone on there before."

The trouble began with his youngest son, Jordan, who had been diagnosed some years earlier with a severe form of Attention Deficit Disorder (ADD). His condition had worsened over the years and now at the age of twelve his behavior was strongly negative.

"I had recently remarried and Jordan wasn't accepting his four-year-old stepsister," Jimmy tells. "It got to the point where he was hurting her physically and even wishing she would die. He kept denying it, but we finally discovered the truth."

To ease the tension, Jordan was sent to spend some time with his grandmother. While there, a very startling problem became evident. Jordan wanted in the worst way to return home and keep the peace with his stepsister, but as soon as his thoughts turned to working that out, his nights became unbearable.

He began having trouble sleeping, not because he wasn't used to the strange house or the strange bed, but because he was being visited by dark and eerie strangers from another dimension.

"They were about of average height, pudgy, and charcoal black in appearance, like they had been cleaning chimneys, or maybe burned," Jordan remembers. "They would visit me when I was trying to go to sleep. And they wouldn't leave me alone."

The entities had one thing on their minds: to create chaos for young Jordan Lowery and his family.

He remembers their threats very well.

"They told me that as long as I was mean to my stepsister and anyone else who got in my way, they would leave me alone. But if I didn't do what they wanted, they would come every night and bother me."

The eerie visitors also told Jordan that if he ever told anyone, he would pay severely. It took two years for him to gain the confidence to tell his father.

"And that's how it was, night after night," Jordan remembers. "Three black entities with red eyes would stand in a line at the foot of my bed, sending negative messages into my head."

Jimmy Lowery believed that it was time to take his son to a counselor or psychiatrist. But with his own counseling background and the remembrance of his own experiences, he knew something else was going on.

"Finally, I realized that Jordan had been involved with something evil, something he wouldn't discuss with me. Something had been happening in our previous house, and I now wondered if it hadn't followed us here."

This brought back vivid memories to Jimmy Lowery, of his early childhood and a lesson he had learned that would help him later in life.

II

In 1969 Jimmy was five years old, with an active interest in all things unusual. His first introduction to the Ouija board came at a dinner party. His father was a pastor in Mississippi, and a member of his congregation, a woman in her fifties, invited the family for an evening of fun. After the meal, the hostess suggested they play the Ouija.

"My parents had heard of the Ouija, something popular, that everyone considered a harmless game, but none of us realized what it could do."

Jimmy and his parents, along with the hostess, began to pose questions to the board, asking for information on the outcome of an upcoming football game and the fate of a family member in Vietnam, among other things.

"I remember the board telling my mother that my favorite uncle would return from the war safely, with a minor injury—which he did. He was in good health, having suffered a slight shrapnel wound. And we also learned that the football game turned out as the board said, complete with the final score."

The only thing the board didn't tell the whole truth about was Jimmy's mother, who it said would become pregnant with a baby boy. The baby was miscarried two months into the pregnancy.

"That thing sure made me curious," Jimmy remembers. "I began doing research into this game and learned some startling things. There is nothing 'playful' about those boards. They pull you into an addiction to the game, a slow but sure means of mind control."

Jimmy thought more about his early life as he worked to understand his son's visits form the night strangers. Then came a night that none of them will ever forget or entirely understand, when the old house in Graham, Texas, came alive with a horror unmatched in Jimmy Lowery's life.

He and his wife at that time, Marsha, had gone to bed, and the kids had settled into sleep in their own bedrooms, when footsteps sounded on the back porch. The footsteps progressed from the porch into the kitchen, and the lights suddenly popped on.

They lay in bed, thinking one of the two kids had gotten up for a snack.

When Jimmy asked who was up, both children answered that they were in bed.

So then, who was in the house?

The two family dogs, both large and formidable, growled, but stayed on the floor at the foot of the bed.

Jimmy took a pistol from his bedroom and, after opening the bedroom door, crept cautiously toward the kitchen. He found no one there. Nor was there anyone visible in any other part of the house.

"I turned the light off and went back to bed," Jimmy remembers. "I left the door ajar so I could see out. I had just begun to relax when the kitchen light came back on. This time, the two dogs went crazy."

The dogs pranced and growled, jumping up on the bed, and then down, the hair on their backs standing straight up, while Jimmy and Marsha looked on in shock.

"I had never seen them this way," Jimmy recalls. "I was quite unnerved."

The light in the kitchen went off and the dining-room

lights burst on, bringing the two kids from their beds into their parents' bedroom.

"I knew for certain that whatever was in the house couldn't be human," Jimmy says. "I knew we were facing something evil. The feeling was all over the house."

Taking his pistol again, more for a feeling of security than actual protection, Jimmy Lowery searched the house. He began to feel guilty for having fallen back in his efforts to remain tied to his Christian teachings, and for over an hour he pondered his predicament and just what it was that had invaded their home.

"I knew that I shouldn't have drifted so far from what I had been taught as a child," Jimmy says. "I resolved to turn myself around, right then and there."

He stood in his home, looking, listening.

"Everything seemed to calm down," Jimmy remembers. "I got the kids back in their beds and returned to mine with a change of heart, determined to work on my own problems. I settled in, saying prayers to myself, talking with Marsha. We both drifted off to sleep."

Then something awakened Jimmy, and he knew that he wasn't dreaming.

"I heard a voice say, 'Wake up. I have to tell you something.' "

He didn't recognize the voice, and his wife lay fast asleep.

Jimmy tried to move in bed, but felt paralyzed, pinned down by the covers and defenseless.

"Suddenly I could feel this thing hovering over the bed,

telling me it was going to get me. Then it descended down upon me."

Jimmy felt suffocated. He struggled, but still couldn't move. He yelled to be released, but the entity grew only stronger.

"I remember turning my head to tell Marsha to get out of the bed, but it appeared that her head had turned around on her shoulders. I was looking at her back and her face at the same time."

Jimmy was now even more paralyzed. The face he saw was that of a beast, something very horrid and foreign to his consciousness.

"I don't even have the words to describe it," he says. "It kept telling me that it wanted me and would have me, that it was going to take my soul and that no one could stop it."

Jimmy Lowery yelled for God's help and kicked and flailed and broke loose from his paralysis, slamming his fist into the back of his wife's head. But there was no face and no beast, just his wife, who was sleeping peacefully.

She continued to sleep, seemingly not feeling a thing.

"I'll never understand that completely," Jimmy says. "I read the Bible the rest of the night, worrying that I had injured my wife. I couldn't wake her but I didn't see a mark on her, either, and she was breathing normally, sleeping just as peacefully as you please. The next morning she awakened happy and refreshed, not having any memory of anything that had happened."

Jimmy could never bring himself to tell his wife about the incident.

———

Two years later Jimmy had remarried and was settled with Jordan and a young stepdaughter in Clanton, Alabama. Here, Jordan finally admitted that he had been dabbling in the occult, and using a Ouija board.

He had been experimenting for over three years, using it with Marsha, his stepmother, while they had been living in Texas. They had been involved with the board every time his father was gone on Air Force reserve duty.

"I asked him if he had any more use for Ouija boards," Jimmy recalls. "He assured me that he never wanted to see another one again."

Jordan had come to realize that a seemingly harmless game had caused a problem they couldn't get away from.

At some time during their rituals with the board Jordan had been deceived by forces from another dimension. He had been told by the forces that they could give him power and thus aide him to gain control of his surroundings.

"Jordan let them come to him," Jimmy says. "He allowed them through a portal, gave them permission to join him, and then they haunted and tormented him. He got nothing from them but grief and heartache, and hate, which he began taking out on his stepsister."

Jimmy and Jordan both believe that their faith in God was answered by deliverance from the demons. Jimmy's brush with the dark power in the bedroom was a signal that those forces intended to destroy their lives.

Luckily, it didn't happen.

But such forces, placed at bay by strong faith, are not easily turned away.

Not long after, Jimmy was working in the attic when he discovered a Ouija board resting against a two-by-four stud, facing outward. Another struggle ensued; this time, more within Jimmy's mind.

Nothing showed itself and no voices were heard.

Just the strong feeling of evil that can never be stopped.

"I believe that board showed up to say, 'You're not getting rid of us,' " Jimmy says. "I believe that by that time, I had learned to control my fear, and also my anger—the two main things evil feeds upon."

Jimmy burned the board and continues praying that the evil will remain at bay.

Since becoming a man of the cloth, Reverend Lowery has not had to fight the night demon again. Jordan's night visitors have also receded back into the abyss. The young man is still challenged by ADD and will not sleep in the dark.

Reverend Lowery is writing a book about the ordeals of those who fight the night monsters, and has a website, *www.jelm.net*, that tells his own story and the stories of others who have fallen prey to the Ouija board, beseeching those who will listen not to fall into the deceitful trap that awaits all who play the dark game.

The Eyes in the Shadows

I

Double Bar 7 Ranch
Eastern Montana

Along the banks of the Yellowstone River sits a large ranch house that was built well before the turn of the last century and has been occupied by members of the Harmon family ever since. Jackie Harmon, now a young housewife and a fifth-generation horsewoman, knows the family house all too well, and the horror that nearly took her mind and her life, horror that she believes may still be trapped within the two-story structure.

No one can say exactly when it began and certainly no one wants to admit that it exists. But Jackie Harmon is certain of what happened to her there.

"It began when I was a senior in high school," she

remembers. "I can't even say what started it all, just that it started."

Jackie became aware of a presence in her room late one night after returning from a football game. As she lay in bed, she had the strange feeling that someone was watching her in the darkness. She turned on the light to see if her little sister, Peggy, might have entered, but she was in her own bed, fast asleep. And so were her parents.

Jackie returned to her bed, but got little sleep the rest of the night.

Two nights later Jackie noticed a strange smell in the room, as if something acrid was burning. She didn't smoke and neither did her friends, and she hadn't used a match for any purpose. It was confusing.

Later that night Jackie again felt a presence in the room and awakened to see some sparkling along the ceiling above her head. She turned on her bedside lamp and looked up.

Nothing.

But as soon as she turned the light off, the sparkling returned.

"I tried to sleep with the light on but I wasn't used to it," Jackie recalls. "I didn't want to awaken my parents, either. My mother, especially, thought I was going through one of those 'teenage things' as she liked to call it. She thought I was half-cracked anyway."

After a week of disturbance and trying to make up her mind that none of it was real, Jackie decided to try to make whatever it was go away.

She thought about it for a while and remembers vividly what happened next.

"I remember talking to my room, in my mind, saying that I wished whatever was happening would stop. And for a couple of nights it did, and I got some sleep. I thought it was all over and I felt good."

But it wasn't all over. Whatever this was returned the following weekend, and this time it was even more disturbing.

"Dad had yelled at me to turn down my stereo," Jackie recalls. "So I just shut it off and went to bed. I must have fallen asleep right away, but then I felt someone touching me on my face."

Jackie thought her father had come into the room. She sat up in the darkness and asked him why he hadn't knocked, then realized that whoever it was standing beside her bed was someone, or something, that she couldn't see.

She also wondered why she might have thought it was her father. She couldn't remember him ever touching her face before, at any time. He would tousle her hair occasionally when she was younger, but nothing like the cold feeling she had just felt against her cheek.

"I was really frightened and turned all my lights and my stereo back on. Then my father did come to the door."

Jackie asked him if he had been in her room and he said that he hadn't but that he wished she would turn her stereo down. He didn't seem to want to stay and talk, so Jackie asked if her mother would come to her room.

"I talked with my mother and told her that I had been hearing things in the room," Jackie remembers. "I couldn't help myself. I just had to tell someone. She asked if I had been drinking, smelled my breath, and warned me that drugs and alcohol weren't good. I already knew that, so I said I was likely having nightmares."

No sooner had Jackie's mother left the room than the lights went out all over the house. Jackie sat on the edge of the bed, petrified. She didn't want to disturb her parents again; they had already taken her little sister into their bedroom.

So she sat in the darkness, wondering what to do. Then she heard just the faintest sound—a low, deep laughing.

She couldn't move. She sat rigid as stone while the low laughing continued. Then, the laughing stopped, just before the lights came back on, and she heard someone call her name.

"It wasn't a voice I'd ever heard before," Jackie remembers. "It was low and kind of gravelly. I'll never forget that voice."

II

Jackie Harmon was now convinced that she was going crazy, living within a horror movie, only much worse than any Hollywood production she had ever watched.

"It was all so subtle," Jackie says. "It was like I wanted to believe it was my imagination when I knew for certain that it wasn't. And when I heard the laughing, and my name called out, I realized that something evil was happening. I really didn't want to face it on my own."

The disturbances continued and the force in her room grew ever bolder. Often Jackie would awaken to someone, or something, jumping on her bed. Whatever it was didn't stay long, just bounced a few times and was gone.

Then late one night the sparkling returned and as Jackie watched it, praying to herself, the little bursts of light came together along the ceiling to form a hooded figure with a huge batlike head and two glowing red eyes.

"I absolutely couldn't move," Jackie remembers. "I just stared at this black, smarmy thing that hovered over the bed, its eyes watching me. I thought I was going to die."

The hooded figure became small lights again, and when Jackie was finally able to move, she left her room and silently made her way out of the house and sat down on the lawn to cry.

The next day she talked with her friends at school about it. It seemed they had already figured out that something more than boyfriend problems had been troubling her.

"At first I worried that they would think I was crazy," Jackie remembers. "But they didn't. One of them said her parents had gotten rid of a ghost by telling it to leave."

Jackie wondered if such an approach might work for her. That night she climbed into bed and when the sparkling light appeared, she told it to go away. She even went as far as to tell it that nothing about it was real.

"I realized just as soon as I said it what a mistake I had made," Jackie recalls. "I didn't have trouble getting to sleep, but what happened to me after that scared me so badly I couldn't talk for nearly fifteen minutes."

Jackie awakened feeling suffocated and unable to

breathe as if a large presence had climbed on top of her. She struggled and couldn't move until, finally, she got her arms loose from the bed.

"I tried to push this weight off me," Jackie recalls, "and I could actually feel a large body covered with coarse, bristly hair."

Jackie couldn't move her mouth, but lurched and screamed within her mind and struggled to get out of bed. The hairy presence finally lifted and she rolled onto the floor, gasping for breath. Her parents came rushing in, and though Jackie couldn't speak at first, she realized that they, too, smelled the strong odor of bad breath in the room.

"They knew it wasn't marijuana," Jackie says, "but they couldn't understand what it was. I couldn't tell them, I just couldn't."

The next morning Jackie's mother suggested they make an appointment with a therapist. Jackie persuaded her to wait awhile, that things would be fine.

Meanwhile, Jackie got busy trying to find help.

"I told my friends that what I had in my room was more than just a ghost," Jackie tells. "I told them what was happening and, in fact, one of my friends knew a girl in a nearby town who had had a similar experience."

III

That Saturday night Jackie and her friends drove to the nearby town. Along the way, they became frightened at anything and everything. After waiting a short time in a small café, Jackie's friend pointed out the window. The girl had arrived with her friends.

They all drove to the girl's home, where they went upstairs into the girl's room. No one else was home, so they all felt able to speak freely.

"This girl told me that the devil had come to live with her," Jackie recalls. "She said it so matter-of-factly, adding that she must have been very bad for that to happen and that even after a priest had come to bless the house, there was still trouble."

Apparently the trouble wasn't as escalated as it had been before. The girl told Jackie that there was no longer any danger of her books and pencils flying around the room, and that she no longer had visions of blood smeared on the walls or in the shower.

"There were rumors that someone had been murdered in the house way back in the 1920s or '30s," Jackie tells. "I know nothing like that ever happened in our house, so I couldn't see any connection."

And, similar to Jackie's situation, her parents hadn't been all that concerned, until the night the house had caught on fire.

"This girl said that they were in the living room, watching television, when the curtains went up in flames," Jackie tells. "When they jumped up to call 911, the fire went out. It hadn't even been a real fire. That's when they called the priest."

That night Jackie got the name of the priest who had come to the home. She realized that it was the priest from her own town, the parish where she and her family regularly attended mass.

"I decided that he must be an exorcist or something," Jackie tells. "It turns out that he wasn't. He just happened to know more about such things than other priests in the area."

When the priest arrived, the first thing he did was instruct Jackie to get rid of her heavy metal music. He explained that some minds are more open to suggestion than others, and not that Jackie was more open, but possibly someone who had listened to music with her might have consciously or unconsciously been attracted to the demonic figures on one of the covers.

"He was matter-of-fact about it," Jackie recalls. "He didn't say I was bad or that I had devils in the room. He just said that whether I realized it or not, I could be bringing some of the horror on myself."

Jackie insisted on staying while the priest anointed the room.

"He tossed holy water on the wall to see what would happen. It sizzled. I couldn't believe it, but it sizzled like a hot pan. Then he turned to me and said that I should find another place in the house to sleep until he was finished, and that it might take as much as a week or two."

During that time, Jackie slept with her little sister, who had been kept clear of the happenings. Jackie prayed that the demon in her room wouldn't come to where she slept with Peggy. It didn't, but she could hear growling from time to time, and other noises as well.

"I believe it was attached somehow to my room, and maybe because of something someone did in there in years past," Jackie says. "I was just glad it didn't move all over the house."

Jackie overheard the priest talking with her mother one evening and she watched as her mother went into the attic and came back down with a Ouija board, one she had kept with her since college, but had left stored and had forgotten about.

The priest left with the board and the sounds and tapping and growling diminished gradually, allowing Jackie to move back into her room.

She wondered at first if she would be able to stand being in the dark in the same place where she had worried about dying. But with time, she was able to resume a normal life.

"The priest helped a lot," Jackie recalls. "He told me that evil feeds on fear and anger, and that if a person develops a strong faith in all that's good, God, or whatever you want to call that force, then a person's mind becomes healthy and there's nothing to worry about."

The priest also told Jackie that most young people harbor some anger about their situation in life and that turning to the dark side is a mistake.

"They go in way over their heads, is what he said,"

Jackie recalls. "And the truth is, the evil is making a mockery of them, a victim. After something bad happens, the evil laughs and is gone, leaving the victim to face penalties for whatever they've done."

Jackie says that the last time she saw the girl from the nearby town, now a student in nursing school, they discussed the "devil in her room," as she had termed it, and both came to the conclusion that there are houses and locales where evil has been called in, or has otherwise entered, that will remain tainted, hoping to attach itself to unsuspecting victims. These places cannot be changed, not without the assistance of just the right priest or minister, or a holy man of some kind.

"It has to be the right kind of person," Jackie says. "No doubt about it. Otherwise a person is trapped inside a horror they can never escape."

The Rat Room

I

San Francisco, California

Jake and Jackie Prescott had recently moved to California from Oregon, where he had worked in law enforcement. They had been living in a motel with their two children—Alex, aged nine, and Carley, seven—for nearly a month before finally closing on an older house.

From the outside, the house appeared similar to many others in the neighborhood: a two-story, Victorian design built in the early 1900s, with pillars on the front porch and a white picket fence surrounding the yard.

But all similarities ended there.

Even the terms of purchase took an unusual turn.

At the last minute, the sellers had wanted an additional clause added to the contract, not only to accept the house as is but not to hold them liable if they encountered unusual strangers either inside or outside the house that might cause them trouble.

It seemed an unusual addendum and made Jake wonder if the house had been used by drug dealers in the past. But he knew from his work in law enforcement how to handle such circumstances. He had taken a job as a detective with the San Francisco Police Department.

Despite the fact that the house had been uninhabited for nearly a year, the Prescotts felt lucky to have found a place that suited them so well, for such a good price, and so near to Jake's office. The only drawback appeared to be that the old house needed attention and possibly a good cat that loved to catch mice. It seemed a likely challenge for a young couple with a lot of energy.

The living room and attached kitchen were open and airy, with good lighting from south-facing windows. The two downstairs bedrooms were good-sized, with good lighting as well. But the upstairs was a different matter. The three bedrooms were small and two of them poorly lit. One of the rooms, set off by itself in the northwest corner of the house, had been sadly neglected. Light was provided by a single bare bulb connected to an antiquated socket that worked by means of a twist-style switch. The light dangled awkwardly by a two-strand black wire from the middle of the ceiling.

The Prescotts got the impression that it had been a storage area and had received little upkeep over the years. A badly needed overhaul should fix the problem. In fact, Jackie became excited at the prospect that the room might serve her well for designing and storing her crafts. She could even envision how she wanted it to look.

They signed the contract still thinking that the price was too good to be true. The Realtor had told them that the sellers had been very motivated and needed the money immediately.

Jake and Jackie were eager to get settled. They would use the master bedroom downstairs and give Carley the adjoining room. Then they would immediately begin remodeling the upstairs bedrooms, starting with the one that also faced south.

They would strip the old wallpaper and paint it an off-white. This would be Alex's room, and he was glad to have the privacy.

But as soon as the work began, the house started to change.

Jackie had looked at the house just once, and had felt fine at the time. She had even looked at the small room upstairs, noting a musty smell, but concluding that it was due to the old boxes and clothes scattered throughout. That room had helped them make the decision to buy, so that she would have her own space to work on craft projects.

But now things were different.

"There was something very strange about that house," Jackie recalls. "I came to believe that whatever it was had hidden itself until we moved in. I didn't feel good anywhere, upstairs or down, especially after dark."

Ironically, her worst feelings came from the old room upstairs, the one she had been so eager to remodel and use for a craft room. Despite the fact that the furnace worked well and there was plenty of heat elsewhere in the house, that room stayed very chilly.

No one went in the room much during the first month of their residence. Jake and Jackie spent their time remodeling Alex's room, so that he might be more comfortable. He had been complaining of bad dreams.

"He wouldn't say what they were," Jackie remembers, "just that he couldn't sleep well and that he heard noises coming from the corner room."

Jake and Jackie began to wonder about the noises themselves. They had just gone to bed one evening, after tucking Carley in for the night, and began to hear a thumping sound coming from above the ceiling in the kitchen.

"It was coming from one corner of the ceiling, up against the west wall," Jackie tells. "The surface was uneven and rough, like it had been rebuilt sometime after the house had been constructed. It was behind this wall that we heard the thumping."

The thumping would occur off and on, day or night, without any predictable pattern. Wind blowing trees along the outside of the house was ruled out and Jake finally concluded that there was a loose board behind the wall. He would get to it after the other remodeling was completed.

"That very night, just as soon as Jake said he was not going to tear the wall apart, I saw a young woman in my dreams," Jackie says. "She was blond, with her hair pulled up in a bun. She wore a high-topped dress from the 1800s and she was holding it together at the throat. She was staring at me through the window in the upstairs corner room. Her lips were moving and she was very anxious. I sat up in bed and screamed."

Jake said he would start on the wall in the kitchen just as soon as he got Alex's room completed. He had been very busy with his new detective job and had been working long hours, something Jackie wasn't happy about.

"But what could I say? He was making a living for us and his job required unusual hours. I just didn't like being alone in the house with the kids."

One afternoon while the kids were in school, Jackie decided to begin cleaning up the small upstairs room, thinking that removing a lot of the refuse would cheer everyone up. She removed a few old boxes, dusted off an old dresser, and moved to the small window, then having no idea that her work was disturbing something strange and dormant.

"I was trying to open the window, the one I had seen the woman looking through at me in my dreams, when her face appeared," Jackie tells. "She was crying, holding the collar of her dress tight around her throat."

Jackie jumped back from the window and the image disappeared. She wondered if she had just imagined it, that perhaps her dream had somehow refocused within her mind. But the more she thought about it the more she realized that the vision had been real.

She said nothing to Jake about it when he came home, but the afternoon's experience was driven home solidly that night when she and Jake heard the thumping in the wall once again. This time louder and for a longer duration.

They didn't bother to get up and look, but Jackie knew that she was seeing a spirit in her mind and that it wanted something from her.

She didn't know what the thumping meant, unless the spirit was trying to get her attention in that way as well. The thought of it troubled her, but she still kept it secret from Jake.

In addition, that same night, Alex came down the stairs and said that he had seen a rat cross in front of his door. He admitted that he had been up late, with a light on near his bed, listening to music through his headphones, when he had seen the rat. His door had been partly ajar and he had seen it scamper past.

Jake took a flashlight and a baseball bat to investigate. He found nothing.

"I even looked for droppings," he said. "Couldn't find a thing."

Jake thought that perhaps Alex had seen a mouse, as there were still a few in the house that hadn't been trapped. But Alex insisted that he knew the difference between the two species and was upset that they wouldn't believe him.

Following the incident, Carley climbed into bed with Jake and Jackie and Alex went into his sister's bed. Jake and Jackie lay awake, discussing what was happening upstairs, wondering what Alex had seen, when Alex came in and asked them if they could hear anything. Jake made another trip upstairs, only to find absolutely nothing. He returned and allowed Alex to roll out a sleeping bag on their floor.

No one slept the remainder of the night. The thumping

in the wall had stopped. They all lay awake, listening instead
to scratching noises coming from the corner room upstairs.

II

The following night Alex returned to his room and there
were no more rats for the following three weeks. The
thumping in the kitchen wall had diminished as well and
everyone relaxed.

Jake had been working long hours on a case and decided to take a few days off to rest and get some more work
done inside the house. Alex's room was finished and perhaps their problems with noises would vanish altogether
once the small room upstairs was remodeled.

Jake and Jackie drew out the plans for her craft room.
Jake decided to begin by replacing the old light. After turning off the breaker, he placed a ladder in the middle of the
room and prepared to rewire a new light fixture into the
ceiling.

As soon as he touched the cord, he got a heavy jolt of
electricity.

"I've been shocked before," he tells, "but nothing like
that. There was a lot of current there, more than there
should have been, and it held me fast. I stumbled off the
ladder and was hanging from the ceiling. At least that's what
my wife said. I don't remember."

Jackie heard a strange moaning coming from upstairs and hurried up to see Jake swinging from the ceiling, his hand wrapped around the light switch. As soon as she entered the room, he fell to the floor.

"The room was filled with a strange haze," Jackie remembers. "Kind of gray and thick. I ran to Jake and he was laughing. His arm from the wrist to his elbow was black, but he said that it didn't hurt. I couldn't understand it."

Jackie wanted to call an ambulance, but Jake talked her out of it. He felt embarrassed by the situation and didn't want to be teased by his fellow detectives.

"I know that I shut the breaker off," he says. "In fact, I checked it again and the switch was still in the off position, and the breaker was fine."

Jake proceeded with the utmost caution. Everything went well. He installed the new light fixture with no problems.

"I was so scared," Jackie remembers. "I told him to just forget it, but he didn't want to be beaten. I thought his macho attitude was foolish and we argued. But he went ahead anyway and then told me that he had been right. Somewhere deep inside, I knew better."

Jake was called back to his case and began working late hours again. Jackie's fear rose and the third night he was gone, the thumping began anew, and Alex saw the rat again. It sat just outside his door and stared in at him. He crawled under the covers and when he finally emerged, the rat was gone.

"He was scared to death," Jackie remembers. "I let him stay in Carley's room and she slept with me every night. Jake said he would sleep upstairs just to see what all the fuss was about. He didn't like the idea of me catering to the kids, and we argued about that."

Jake saw nothing and insisted that everyone was over-reacting. But he did notice that the small room changed from hot to cold, and back to hot, when he stood inside one evening.

One evening, while Jake was working, Jackie had an especially vivid dream. The young woman was back and her collar was open revealing a neck that was swollen and discolored. She was again looking through the window, and as Jackie struggled to open it, the woman held up a letter.

Jackie couldn't get the window open and the spirit couldn't hold the letter still enough for her to read. She awakened with a start, finding her daughter talking to her.

"Carley said that a lady had been standing beside the bed," Jackie recalls. "She said that the lady had been crying and holding her neck."

Jackie insisted that they move from the house, but Jake argued that they had used a lot of savings up renovating the house, and that they still had a long way to go. He suggested they call in someone from his department, a woman named Marlene Cox, who specialized in occult crime. This person might have some answers.

The night before Marlene Cox arrived, Alex came down the stairs and said that he had seen the rat again, inside his room this time, and that it was even bigger than either of the previous times. Jake went up with a flashlight and his pistol.

Jackie followed him, worried that he might need help. He insisted that he didn't, but having her along made him realize that what they both saw together was real, and the most terrifying thing either of them had ever encountered.

They entered the room, Jake in the lead. He reached for the light switch and they both jumped at a loud hissing sound coming from the corner. Jake trained his flashlight on a huge rat that sat, impossibly, on the side of the closet.

"It was bigger than any dog I've ever seen," Jake said, "and it stared at us with red eyes. It was sitting perpendicular to the room, which just couldn't happen. But we both saw it."

They stumbled out of the room and once downstairs, Jake got his pistol and returned to the room. Jackie begged him not to go, but he went anyway, determined to rid them of the horrible creature, whatever it was.

"I just knew that it wasn't really a rat," Jackie tells. "It just couldn't be, not and be that size and sitting sideways on the door of the closet."

When Jake entered the room, he again heard the hissing. But before he could fire, the rat disappeared, melting into the closet door.

"That's the only way I can describe it," Jake tells. "It was as if that thing were chocolate, or something, that instantly became part of the door. I listened to Jackie this time and we packed some clothes and left, that very night."

***

Jackie never went back inside the house again. She allowed Jake to make all the arrangements to have their furniture and other personal items moved into storage, while they took residence in an apartment and put the house up for sale.

Though Jake said nothing about their experiences with the rat, Marlene Cox insisted on seeing the house. She had done an investigation and had learned some interesting things that the Realtor had somehow forgotten to mention.

"Marlene and I went back into the room and began to look closely at the closet and its interior," Jake says. "We stripped off some wallpaper and some siding and discovered where there had been an old doorway and a set of stairs that had led down into the kitchen. The new wall in the kitchen had been constructed a number of years before to block off the stairwell. It seems a woman had hanged herself in there for some reason."

Jackie now realized that the woman she had seen in her dreams and who had come to the foot of her bed had to be that woman, and that the thumping noises had to be the sounds of her feet kicking the walls in her death throes. She had been hanging herself over and over again in the stairwell.

Marlene Cox had an explanation for the rat. After tearing some wallpaper loose in the room, she discovered various occult symbols and markings, indicating that some form of black magic had been performed in the room. Though she dealt entirely with concrete evidence where her cases were concerned, she said that she often encoun-

tered elements of paranormal activity that couldn't be explained in criminal terms.

"She thought that perhaps the rat was a demonic presence that could have preceded the young woman having
moved in," Jake tells. "Something happened in the house
to cause the young woman's despair and that the evil presence might have worked to pull her deeper and deeper into
depression. In the end, she was pulled into suicide."

Jake and Jackie Prescott still live in the apartment complex
and are striving to regain their losses from the house. It still
hasn't sold and they recently filed suit against the Realtor
for misrepresenting the property. Their case is pending.

Screaming in the Rain

I

Big Belt Mountains
Helena, Montana

Outside of Montana's capital city lies vast amounts of natural wilderness, forested areas that encompass thousands of acres. Few roads traverse this rugged terrain and anyone who ventures there should be prepared for the worst.

Leslie Malone had grown up farther north, in the Missoula area, and was an avid hiker and outdoors enthusiast. She never left home without being prepared for all kinds of weather.

But during a weekend trip in October of 1987, she had no way of knowing what awaited her and her friends along a lonely stretch of gravel road deep in the Big Belt Mountains.

She was traveling with her boyfriend, Jeff Marks, and

three other companions, all on an outing to do some back-packing after attending a small-town football game in Har-lowton, a good three hours from Helena, where Leslie worked in a sporting goods store. Jeff had a younger brother playing on the visiting team and everyone thought it would be fun to relive some high school memories and have a good time in the mountains, all during the same weekend.

Their plan was to spend the afternoon boating at Canyon Ferry Lake and then take a gravel road through the mountains and stay the night at White Sulpher Springs, a small town along the way. Jeff had a sturdy SUV and everyone fit into the vehicle easily, even with the tents and camping gear packed in the back. It seemed that a good time would be had by all.

But the afternoon at Canyon Ferry proved to be the beginning of a bad weekend, as one of the group, a college student named Gary, nearly drowned waterskiing. Together, Leslie and her friend Janelle saved him and they felt relieved at having avoided a tragedy without involving the author-ities.

But this event caused them to get a late start over the mountains. In addition, a heavy bank of clouds rolled in and a steady rain began falling, making the driving ex-tremely difficult. As darkness approached, it became obvi-ous that they would not reach White Sulpher Springs without taking perilous chances along the way. So the group decided collectively to make camp and get an early start the next morning.

They found a forest service campground along a stream.

The rain worsened and they erected their two tents with difficulty, sharing one flashlight that Jeff had brought along. Adding to everyone's disappointment was the fact that they couldn't build a fire to dry out. They would change clothes inside the tents and huddle inside their sleeping bags, while Leslie cooked hamburgers over a small camp stove that Jeff always kept in his vehicle.

"We were really cramped in that one tent, so the other three went back over to Gary's tent while Jeff and I cooked," Leslie remembers. "They would come back over once the food was ready."

Inside the other tent, Gary's girlfriend, Molly, pulled a Ouija board from her backpack. Leslie's friend, Janelle, became uneasy immediately. She recalled a party three weeks previous where Molly had been playing with some other friends and the lights had gone out. Leslie had been at the same party and prior to their trip had made Molly promise to leave the Ouija board at home.

"Leslie didn't like Molly all that well, anyway," Janelle recalls. "It was complicated, because Jeff and Gary were good friends."

Janelle reminded Molly of her promise to Leslie. This had no effect on Molly. Instead, she insisted that what she wanted to do would just take a minute, and begged her not to tell Leslie. So Janelle gave in, something she regrets to this day.

"If I'd known what was going on," Janelle says, "I would have insisted that she put the board away immediately."

She gave in because Molly insisted that she needed to finish something that would make the trip easier for all of them.

Janelle remained on the edge. To complicate things, Gary was still physically ill from his brush with death and lay moaning in his sleeping bag. Though Molly seemed unconcerned, Janelle worried about him. It seemed he was getting sicker. He had been vomiting off and on during the trip into the mountains, but hadn't been moaning.

Molly placed the board on the tent floor while Janelle sat to one side and insisted that she hurry. Something about the board seemed to change the interior of the tent.

"I was already weirded out from that afternoon," Janelle recalls. "I mean, Gary was dead. Leslie and I worked on him for a long time. I don't know how he came back."

Janelle suggested she forget the game until after the meal, but Molly insisted on continuing, rubbing her hands all over the board and saying something in a low tone.

"I think she'd gotten addicted to it," Janelle recalls. "Everything about that whole night was so strange. I had changed clothes and was shivering like mad, but Molly sat there in just her bra and panties. I mean, we could see our breath."

Molly finished her ode to the board and turned to Janelle.

"She asked me to promise that I would never reveal what was about to happen," Janelle remembers. "I told her I couldn't make that promise and she told me that I would be sorry."

II

Janelle asked Molly what she meant by "She would be sorry," and waited for an answer. She finally realized that whoever she was talking to no longer even seemed like Molly.

"She appeared to be somebody else," Janelle recalls. "She had even taken on a kind of masculine appearance. She kept talking about Marco. So I asked her who Marco was and she turned to me with this strange look in her eyes. She said that Marco had been following her around for the past two weeks, ever since she had contacted him at the party in Helena."

Molly turned back to the board and Janelle decided to get up and leave.

But she couldn't.

"I was held down somehow," Janelle recalls. "I couldn't move. The air felt heavy and thick, almost like Jell-O."

Janelle could hear herself telling Molly to stop. But it was only in her head. No words would come out, just the protesting within.

She watched helplessly as Molly doubled over and kissed the board, then began with a series of questions.

Molly's first question dealt with the spirit named Marco asking if he might be present.

The board said, yes, he was there.

Molly wanted to know if he, Marco, had been at the lake when Gary almost died.

Another yes.

After another question to the board, dealing with Marco's presence, Molly moved over beside Gary and began choking him.

Something in the tent changed and Janelle then managed to break her own trance. She managed to pull Molly away from Gary.

"We were both screaming and yelling," Janelle recalls. "And then I saw the eyepiece rise off the board and hover like some kind of miniature UFO. It flew into the side of the tent, just missing my head, and began bouncing around everywhere."

Janelle scrambled to get outside. Molly, afraid that Leslie would learn about the board, struggled to hold her back. They kicked and punched and fought, knocking the tent over.

The commotion brought Leslie and Jeff over from the other tent. They managed to untangle everyone, including Gary, who was violently ill.

Jeff helped Gary off to one side, where he vomited for a considerable period of time.

Molly followed them, wrapped in a blanket, avoiding Leslie at all costs.

Leslie recalls being very angry when she heard Janelle's story.

"I knew that Molly was becoming strange because of that board. She had promised me over and over to leave the damned thing at home. Because of her lies we were all having to suffer. I just didn't realize that it was going to get a whole lot worse."

They struggled in the downpour to get the tent erected again. Though they looked everywhere, they couldn't find the Ouija board.

"It was dark and raining like crazy," Leslie explains, "but that board should have been right there with all the other stuff inside the fallen tent. It didn't make sense, and it bothered me a lot."

After a heated exchange, Leslie and Molly went into their separate tents. Jeff insisted that Gary stay with them, which angered Molly. She had no choice but to comply with his wishes.

Janelle wasn't happy about being left in the second tent with Molly.

"Even though I didn't want to believe what had just happened, I had to accept it," she remembers. "And Molly was just so upset that I thought we'd get into another fight right away."

The fight never happened. Molly suddenly dropped the blanket from around herself and rushed out of the tent.

III

Janelle waited for Molly to come back into the tent. After a few minutes, she looked out and began calling for her.

"I should have tried to stop her right away," Janelle remembers. "But I didn't think she would stay out there.

It was still raining hard, mixed with a little snow, and it was cold. Without clothes, she should have just stayed inside."

But then Janelle realized that Molly wasn't thinking clearly, and hadn't been during the entire trip.

She stepped outside in the rain and began calling for Molly. She got no answer. She went over to Leslie and Jeff's tent, where the two of them had stuck their heads out.

"Janelle told me that Molly had left, just taken off somewhere," Leslie recalls. "I knew right then that we might have had some trouble earlier, but we hadn't seen anything yet."

Leslie stayed with Gary, who was still very ill, while Jeff and Janelle bundled themselves up in coats and hats and went into the storm to look for Molly. They worried that Molly might fall into the creek and even if she avoided that, in a very short time she would become a victim of hypothermia. If that happened, she could easily die before they found her.

"We shouted until we were hoarse," Janelle recalls. "We had left Jeff's SUV lights on and thought we'd find Molly soon enough to get back there and turn them off. But we couldn't find her anywhere and wondered if she was already unconscious, or just hiding from us."

After more searching, Jeff and Janelle spread out to cover more ground, keeping in constant touch by voice. Janelle stayed close to the creek while Jeff wandered through the forest. They had walk slowly and carefully in the darkness, with little hope of seeing Molly even if she were right in front of them.

Janelle suddenly felt a surge of hope. Jeff yelled that he

had found Molly and that Janelle should go back to camp to turn his lights off and bring Leslie back.

"Jeff wanted me to assure Leslie that we were both okay and that he would need some warm soup for Molly," Janelle remembers.

Janelle began her walk back toward camp, following a trail that she and Jeff had taken along the creek. Partway back, she heard Jeff calling for Molly, his voice slight and faded in the distance.

"It scared me a lot," Janelle remembers. "I thought he said that he had found her and now I was hearing him calling for her. It was all too weird."

Janelle decided there was no sense in going back to find Jeff, not until she had reached camp first and talked to Leslie.

She continued walking for some time, thinking she should have reached camp.

"I had a feeling that something wasn't right," she remembers. "I could have sworn I should have reached the tents. But I decided I was just confused, wanting to hurry through the rain and worrying about Jeff and Molly. It was a nightmare."

Janelle then noticed a light through the trees. Again, she became confused. She knew that the camp was along the creek and wondered why the headlights would appear from somewhere within the forest.

Then she realized that what she was seeing wasn't a set of headlights, but a single, yellowish glow.

"I thought that it was Molly," Janelle tells. "I thought she had taken one of the lanterns from the tent and was trying to find her way back to camp. So I went toward the glowing light."

Almost too late, she discovered her mistake.

As she struggled through the trees and thick growth, Janelle realized that Molly hadn't taken a lantern with her. She had just burst out, rushing nearly naked into the storm.

Besides that, Jeff had said he located her farther back. Nothing made sense, and she was getting very cold.

She turned around and started back toward the creek, worrying that she would become lost. Then she did see the lights of Jeff's vehicle.

IV

Janelle felt a surge of relief at seeing Jeff's vehicle and the tents.

"I found my way into camp and gave Jeff's message to Leslie. I thought she would be glad to learn we had found Molly. But I didn't know at the time what had been happening in camp."

While Janelle and Jeff had been out searching, Leslie and Gary had been living a strange and horrible nightmare.

"I remember seeing Janelle come into the tent," Leslie tells. "She seemed relieved, thinking it was all over. I had to tell her that Molly had been back in camp for a long time, that she was in the other tent."

Leslie had tried to call out to Jeff and Janelle, but they hadn't heard her.

Utterly confused, Janelle followed Leslie over to the other tent and found that the flap was tied shut.

Molly was enraged and wouldn't let anyone inside.

After calling unsuccessfully for her to open the flap, Leslie and Janelle decided to pull the tent over.

"I leaned over to take one of the stakes out," Leslie recalls, "and a knife blade came through the canvas. It wasn't right in my face, but close enough that I knew not to try and take the tent down."

Leslie and Janelle backed away. From inside came a strange and hideous laugh.

Somehow, Molly had found the Ouiji board and was again asking it questions.

Back in Jeff and Leslie's tent, Leslie began to gradually break down. Jeff was still gone, Molly was insane, and Gary had gotten violently ill again.

"I didn't know what to do," Leslie recalls. "I had never been faced with such a strange situation. My boyfriend was out risking his life for a girl who was obviously possessed by a demon, her boyfriend was dying, and I couldn't do a thing about any of it."

Jeff appeared at the tent flap, shivering from the cold. Leslie broke down in tears and hugged him tightly. But he wasn't in a good mood. He had heard Molly yelling in the next tent and he said that he'd had enough for one night.

"I tried to tell him that she had a knife but he was determined to stop the madness," Leslie remembers. "He went over there and tore that tent off the ground and when Molly came at him, he tackled her and took the knife away. It wasn't easy, because she seemed to have a lot of strength, but Jeff wasn't going to take any more."

Leslie and Janelle assisted Jeff in tying Molly securely with rope from his vehicle. She kicked and screamed and spat at them, calling them every vile name any of them had ever heard, and a few more.

"I had never seen her, or anyone else for that matter, act that way, or make those kinds of sounds," Leslie says. "It was unreal."

Jeff dragged Molly to a tree and reinforced the ropes with a towrope from his vehicle, wrapping it around her and securing it to the back of his bumper. Molly, or whoever she was, would not be allowed to escape.

Jeff then explained that when he had sent Janelle back, he had been certain he had discovered Molly on the ground. But it had only been a strange rock formation, a trick played on the eyes. He added that a strange mist had lingered in the air.

Now that they had Molly, Jeff wasn't going to allow her any freedom. He took the Ouija board and, after filling one of the coolers with water, immersed the board and closed the lid.

They all watched the cooler for a time. Nothing happened.

Having worn herself out, Molly had collapsed. Jeff carried her into their tent and laid her beside Gary.

The following morning, after little sleep, they left for Harlowton. Gary was still sick and Molly was still a limp rag. There was a lot of discussion about just forgetting the football game and everyone going back home, but Jeff had promised his brother he would watch him play.

Along the way, they stopped briefly at a fishing access site along the Musselshell River. Jeff took the Ouija board out of the cooler of water and threw it out into the current.

"Jeff had learned that American Indians get rid of negative articles by placing them in water, which neutralizes the force," Leslie explains. "When we threw that thing in the river it looked like it was trying to swim, or something. It moved around and flipped over, but couldn't stay above the surface. It was very strange and very scary. Molly cried the entire time, but as soon as the board stayed down, she stopped crying. She had a difficult time remembering anything that had happened."

Gary was not so lucky. He still suffers from nightmares and often awakens with a feeling that someone is after him. He avoids lakes and streams, believing somehow that whatever pulled him under in Canyon Ferry is a force that will always be after him.

"He wishes that we had burned the board instead of throwing it in the water," Leslie says. "He thinks he's trapped forever now by whatever came through in that house in Helena."

Index

Air, changes in texture and demonic
    presence, 166, 177, 184
Alaska
    Chilkoot Trail haunting, 30–40
    gold rush, 28, 29
    past life experience in, 10, 33–40
    Skagway, 28, 29, 30
Animals
    crow, as spirit animal, 109–16
    domestic pets, reaction to spirit
      entities, 62, 139
    owl, shape-shifting into and out
      of body journey, 126–28
    rat, demonic, 164–65, 166, 167–
      70
Arabia, past life in, 26
Arizona State University, 107–8

Big Belt Mountains, Idaho,
    demonic possession in, 173–75
Big Lost River, Idaho, 55
Bottoms, Frank and Sylvia, 46, 49,
    50

Bridges, Mark, 22
Bridges, Sally, 21–22, 27–40

Calamity Jane (Martha Jane
    Cannary), 99–104
    spirit appears to Joyce Thierer,
      102–4
Children
    clairvoyance of, 43, 46
    dreams of, 16–18, 27, 31, 44
    past lives and, 16
    spirit friend of, 44
    vulnerable to demons, 59–73,
      136–37, 147–56, 174
Civil War, past life regression and,
    24–26
Coffeeville, Kansas, 99–102
Cox, Marlene, 167–70
Crow, Charlie, 37–39

Dead Man's Hand (cards), 100
Death. *See also* NDE (near-death
    experience)

Index

Death (*continued*)
 other side, depiction of, 25–26,
  44–45
 passing over, 24–26, 44
 spirits visible, 25, 45
 sudden, and restless spirit, 59–73
Demons and demonology
 air, changes in texture, and, 166,
  177, 184
 appearance of demonic figure, 68–
  69, 136
 on camping trip, Big Belt
  Mountains, Helena, Montana,
  175–85
 children and teens vulnerable to,
  59–73, 136–37, 147–56, 174
 disposal of objects associated
  with, 71, 155, 185
 dogs, reaction to, 139
 exorcism of, 154–55
 Graham, Texas, haunted house
  and, 136–43
 heavy metal music and, 154
 "Marco," malevolent spirit, 177
 odors accompanying demonic
  figures, 68, 70, 84, 148
 Ouija board and, 9, 142–43, 175–
  85
 rat, demonic, 164–65, 166, 167–
  70
 voice of, 140, 150, 183
Devil, 153–54, 156. *See also*
  Demons and demonology
Disposal of objects associated with
  evil or spirits, 71, 155, 185
Doorways and portals, to Other
  World
 heavy metal music and, 154
 Native-American mysticism and,
  115–16
 Ouija board and, 9, 142, 155,
  175–85
Double Bar 7 Ranch, Eastern
  Montana, demonic presence,
  147–56
Dreams
 children's, 16–18, 27, 31, 44
 controlled by *bruja*, 29–30

dead appearing in, 66–67, 162–63
 meaning of, 8–9
 nightmare of near-drowning
  victim, 185
 past lives and, 16–17
 snow dreams, 16–17, 19, 27, 31
 spirits, Native American, present
  in, 111–14
 vision and foreboding in, 34–35

Edmonds, Carmen Garcia, 119–30
 debt owed by, to witch, 129–30
 Indian/Spanish heritage of, 119
 shape-shifting into owl and out
  of body journey, 126–28
 visits a witch (*bruja*), 122–23, 125–
  26
Edmonds, Richard, 119–21, 123–
  25, 129
El Paso, Texas, John Wesley Hardin
  and, 79, 83, 85
Ellerman, Amy, 59–73
 destruction of objects associated
  with brother and demonology,
  71–72
 dreams of, 66, 67
 opposition to involvement in
  occult and demonic activity, 72
 possession of, by brother, 67–68
 sighting of brother's spirit, 62, 68
 sighting of demonic figure, 68–70
Ellerman, Eileen, 60, 62, 64–71
 demon notebook found by, 70–71
 depression of, 64, 68
 disturbed behavior by, 65, 67, 68
 suicide attempt, 69
Ellerman, Zackery, 59–73
 death of, 59
 demonology and, 70–73
 eccentric/disturbing behavior, 61
 garden of, 60, 61–62, 64, 68–69,
  71, 73
 haunting by, 61–73
 notebook of, 70–71
Evil, 82, 137, 140, 143, 150, 155–
  56. *See also* Demons and
  demonology
Exorcism, 154–55

Index

Fear
  of demon/devil, 148, 149
  evil feeding on, 155
  of ghosts, 62
  in haunted house, 166
  of nightmares, 16, 19
  of snowstorms, 18
  unknown and, 8–9
  of witch, 126
Fire, set my devil or demon, 153–
  54
France, revolutionary, past life in,
  26

Garcia, Lucio, 119, 123–24, 129
Ghosts. *See* Spirits
Gibson, Bob, 29–34
  past life, 38–39
Gibson, LeAnn, 29–34
Graham, Texas, haunted house, 135–
  43

Hardin, John Wesley, 79–85
  death of author Marohn, 83
  grave site, 80
  haunting of Metz, 81–85
  hundredth anniversary of death,
    80, 83
Harmon, Jackie, 147–56
  arranges exorcism of room, 154–
    55
  consults peer in similar situation,
    153–54
  demonic presence in room, 147,
    148, 149, 151–52, 156
  odor noticed, 148, 152
  Ouija board and, 155
  voice heard, 150
Haunted people
  Christy Matthews, by female
    spirit, 50–55
  Leon Metz by John Wesley
    Hardin, 81–85
Haunted places
  air, changes in texture and, 166,
    177, 184
  Chilkoot Pass, Alaska, 10, 33–40
  houses, 63, 135–43, 159–70

Seaside Point, Portland, Oregon,
  59–73
  temperature changes in, 51, 84,
    162, 167
  Valley of Witches, Colorado, 87–
    95
  West Fork Ranch, Idaho, 47–55
Hickok, Wild Bill, 100
Howard, Oliver O., 48, 54

Ideal Road (Old Spanish Trail),
  Colorado, ghost history, 91
Internet websites opposing occult
  and demonic activities, 72, 143

*John Wesley Hardin: Dark Angel of
  Texas* (Metz), 85

Lights, electric, erratic behavior of,
  139–40
Lights, unexplained or associated
  with spirits
  demonic presence, camping trip,
    Big Butte Mountains,
    Montana, 181
  demonic presence in room of
    Jackie Harmon, 148, 151
  Valley of the Witches, 93–94
Little People (Wee Ones,
  Leprechauns, Trolls, or
  Tommyknockers), 91–93
London, Jack, 16, 17, 30–31
Lowery, Jimmy, 135–43
  attacked by demonic entity, 140–
    41
  Ouija board and, 137–38, 142
  son's ADD and violent behavior,
    136–37
  visits from "night strangers," 138–
    41
  website of, 143

Malone, Leslie, 173–76, 178–85
  demonic possession of companion
    Molly and, 178–85
  disposal of Ouija board and,
    185
  friends fighting on trip, 178

Index

Malone, Leslie (*continued*)
  near-drowning of companion, 174
  Ouija board on trip and demonic
    spirit released by, 177–79
Marks, Jeff, 173–85
Marohn, Richard, 83
Matthews, Christy, 43–55
  dream of, 50
  ghost letter written by, 53
  haunting of, 51–55
  NDE, 44–45, 46
  psychic abilities, 43–44, 46, 47,
    49–50
  spirit friend, 44, 45
Medicine pouch, 124
Metz, Leon, 79–85
  appearance of horsemen, 84
  book title, 81
  mental communication with
    Hardin, 81
  physical and emotional symptoms
    caused by Hardin's haunting,
    82–83, 84–85
  threatened by Hardin, 71
  Spur Award received, 85
Moran, Tom, 107–16
  dreams of old man and crow, 111–
    14
  meeting on Navajo reservation
    with tribal officer and
    discovery of stick with rings,
    108–9
  meeting with old Indian man and
    crow, 109–11
  shape-shifting into crow, 114–15
  spiritual education of, 112–14
  telepathic communication and,
    110
Music, played by ghost, 93–95

Navajo Indian Reservation,
  Northwestern Arizona, 108–11
Native Americans
  disposing of negative objects, 185
  dream instructions and, 111–14
  medicine pouch, 124
  mythology, 9
  Navajo, 108–16

Navajo witches, 125–30
Nez Perce, 48, 54
"other world," 124
shape-shifter, 109–16, 126–29,
  130
spiritualism and mysticism, 9, 108–
  16
witches in, 121–23
NDE (near-death experience), 44–
  45

Object psychometry, 48, 49–50, 52
Other World, 124
Ouija board
  addictive nature of, 138
  camping trip, Big Belt
    Mountains, Helena, Montana
    and, 175–85
  danger of, 9, 143
  demonology and, 9, 142–43, 175–
    85
  fortune-telling with, 137–38
  Graham, Texas, haunted house
    and, 135–43
  "Marco," demonic spirit released
    by, 177–78
Out of body experience, 44, 126–
  28

Past life regressions, 20, 23–27
Past lives, 8
  Carl Reese, 10, 15–40
Place psychometry, 47
Poltergeist-like activity, 162, 163,
  166, 178
Portland State University, 60
Prescott, Jake and Jackie, 159–70
  children of, 159
  colleague in police department
    investigates, 167–70
  house purchase, unusual clause,
    159–60
  near-electrocution of Jake, 165–
    66
  occult symbols in, 169
  rat, demonic, appears, 164–65,
    166, 167–70
  spirit appears, 163, 167, 169

190

spirit appears in dreams, 162–63, 167
thumping in house, 162, 163, 166
upstairs room, 160–62, 163, 165, 167
Psychic ability, clairvoyance, 43–44

Reese, Carl, 15–40
Alaska, attraction to, 15, 20, 21, 27
childhood snow dreams, 16–18, 27, 31
Chilkoot Trail, past life encounter on, 30–40
Civil War battlefield and dying of, 24–27
dying by guillotine in revolutionary France, 26
past life therapy, 23–27
sultan's daughter, past life as, 26
Relationships and past lives, Carl Reese and Bob Gibson, 38–40

San Francisco, California, haunted house, 159–70
San Juan Mountains, New Mexico, witches, 119–30
Selmen, John, 79, 80
Shape-shifting, 109–16, 126–30
Solberg, Martin, 23–24, 27
Soul, past lives and, 8, 26
Spirits (of the dead/ghosts). See also Death
animals' reaction to, 62
attached to place, 47, 50–55, 62–73, 90–95
Calamity Jane, 102–4
Civil War battlefield and, 25–26
communication by, 53, 81
dreams, appearance in, 66–67, 162–63
Ellerman, Zack, haunting by, 61–73
female, Cavalry soldier's wife, 10, 50–55

Johnson, ex-slave, haunting of Valley of Witches, 90–85
malevolent (John Wesley Hardin), 81–85, see also Demons and demonology
movement of objects and, 51, 63, 178
passed over on other side, 45
returning to friends and loved ones, 44
visions of, in wilderness, 28
Spirits (Native-American), 109–16
Story, John, 91–93
Suicide, restless spirits and, 54, 169–70
Symbols in visions and dreams, 44, 45
Synchronicity, 29

Temperature changes, and spiritual entities, 51, 84, 162, 167
Thierer, Joyce, 99–104
spirit of Calamity Jane and, 102–4

University of San Francisco, 21

Valley of Witches, Colorado
accounts of lost treasure, 90
Johnson, ex-slave, story of, 87–95
rumors about, 89–90

West Fork Ranch, Idaho, haunting at, 47–55
Wilson, Paul, 89–95
exploration of Valley of Witches, 90
sighting of strange lights and hearing violin music, 93–95
Witches (brujos and brujas), 122
in Indian country, 130
male, injured while in animal form, 130
shape-shifting into owl and out of body journey, 126–28
visit to, 122–23, 125–26

Yellowstone National Park, 23